WORD
BIBLICAL
THEMES

━━━━━━━━━━━━━━━━━━━━━━━━*General Editor*━━━━━━━━━━━━━━━━━━━━━━━━
David A. Hubbard

━━━━━━━━━━━━━━━━━*Old Testament Editor*━━━━━━━━━━━━━━━━━━━━━
John D. W. Watts

━━━━━━━━━━━━━━━━━*New Testament Editor*━━━━━━━━━━━━━━━━━━
Ralph P. Martin

WORD BIBLICAL THEMES

Micah – Malachi

RALPH L. SMITH

ZONDERVAN
ACADEMIC

To Our Grandsons
Daniel and David Leverenz
Proverbs 17:6

ZONDERVAN ACADEMIC

Micah-Malachi
Copyright © 1990 by Word, Incorporated

Requests for information should be addressed to:
Zondervan, *3900 Sparks Dr. SE, Grand Rapids, Michigan 49546*

ISBN 978-0-310-11514-4 (softcover)

Library of Congress Cataloging-in-Publication Data

Smith, Ralph L.
    Micah-Malachi: Ralph L. Smith.
       p. cm.
    Includes bibliographical references.
    ISBN 978-0-849-90791-3
    1. Bible. O.T. Minor Prophets—Criticism, interpretation, etc. I. Title. II. Series.
BS1560.S66 1990
224'.906—dc20   89-49677

Printed in the United States of America

HB 12.13.2023

CONTENTS

FOREWORD

Finding the great themes of the books of the Bible is essential to the study of God's Word, and to the preaching and teaching of its truths. But these themes or ideas are often like precious gems; they lie beneath the surface and can only be discovered with some difficulty. The large commentaries are useful in this discovery process, but they are not usually designed to help the student trace the important subjects within a given book of Scripture.

The Word Biblical Themes meet this need by bringing together, within a few pages, all of what is contained in a biblical volume on the subjects that are thought to be most significant to that volume. A companion series to the Word Biblical Commentary, these books seek to distill the theological essence of the biblical books as interpreted in the more technical series and to serve it up in ways that will enrich the preaching, teaching, worship, and discipleship of God's people.

In this volume, Ralph Smith draws upon his studies in the minor prophets to present the central themes of Micah-

Malachi. This book is sent forth in the hope that it will contribute to the vitality of God's people, renewed by the Word and the Spirit and ever in need of renewal.

Southern Baptist Theological
Seminary
Louisville, Kentucky

John D. W. Watts
Old Testament Editor
Word Biblical Commentary
Word Biblical Themes

1 INTRODUCTION

The search for biblical themes on an academic level goes back to the works of Gerhard von Rad, "The Form-Critical Problems of the Hexateuch" (1938), and that of Martin Noth, *A History of Pentateuchal Traditions* (1948). Von Rad argued that the Hexateuch is built around six major themes:

- The Primeval History
- The History of the Patriarchs
- The Deliverance from Egypt
- The Divine Revelation at Sinai
- The Wilderness Wanderings
- The Granting of the Land of Canaan.[1]

Martin Noth listed the major themes of the Pentateuch as:

- Guidance out of Egypt
- Guidance into the Arable Land
- Promise to the Patriarchs

- Guidance in the Wilderness
- Revelation at Sinai[2]

These men believed they could identify the Bible's major themes and trace the growth of them. Their work in this regard was confined largely to the Pentateuch or the Hexateuch and used traditio-historical criticism.

The search for biblical themes on a popular level is simpler. It consists of reading the biblical text as it stands, noting the various themes as they arise in context, with a view to understanding the use and meaning of each theme, then and now. Such a procedure keeps one's study anchored to the text, thus resisting any temptation to press the biblical materials into a preconceived theological mold.

Those who read the last seven books of the Minor Prophets (Micah-Malachi) in search of biblical themes encounter an amazing variety of materials. These books contain oracles of judgment and salvation, visions, warnings, disputes, admonitions, songs, hymns, and promises. One might think that a short collection of writings, consisting of only thirty-six chapters and belonging to the same literary genre (prophecy), would be homogeneous and consistent in subject matter and style. But the themes of each book differ greatly, although a basic unity undergirds them.

Micah's themes are concerned with social injustice, judgment, and future hope. Nahum's primary motif is the destruction of Nineveh. Habakkuk was concerned with the presence of evil in the world and God's seeming inactivity. However, the power and presence of evil could not weaken Habakkuk's faith in God's goodness and sovereignty. Zephaniah's primary theme is the coming of world judgment. Haggai and Zechariah were engrossed in the rebuilding of the temple after the return from Babylon. Malachi lived at least a hundred years after the first group of exiles returned to Jerusalem. The high hopes and dreams they had when they returned soon turned to ashes. Discouragement, disappointment, doubt, and skepticism were rife. Malachi tried, with little success, to stem the tide of spiritual lethargy.

Some of the great themes arching over other parts of the Old Testament are scarcely mentioned in these seven books. Such themes as the Exodus, Creation, Sinai, and Covenant are not stressed—although a reader familiar with other parts of the Old Testament may find implications of them. These over-arching themes must have been part of the mental framework of these prophets. What these seven prophets addressed directly, however, were the immediate issues of war and peace, pride, greed, oppression, judgment, the nations, exile, land restoration, and the coming Day of the Lord.

The themes change with the changing times and situations. These writings cover the whole period of classical prophecy from the eighth century B.C. (Micah) to the fifth century B.C. (Malachi). Tremendous changes in the fortunes of the people of God occurred during those years. Samaria, the capital of the Northern Kingdom, fell to the Assyrians in 722 B.C. They sent a large segment of its population into exile in Mesopotamia and brought people from Babylon into Samaria to take their place (2 Kings 17:24). In 586 B.C. Jerusalem fell to the Babylonians. The temple was demolished and burned. A large segment of the population was carried captive to Babylon. In 538 B.C. Cyrus, king of Persia, captured Babylon and issued a decree that the captives in Babylon were free to return to their homes and rebuild their temples. In all these acts of history, the prophets and people of God saw His hand of judgment and mercy.

These seven prophets believed Yahweh had given them messages for their people and their time. As times and circumstances changed, the messages or themes changed. But underneath all the changes and varied themes of these books, the basic unity appears. For example, the covenant

3

name, Yahweh, is used predominately in all seven books. It occurs 280 times in these books, while the name Elohim, "God," is used only 38 times. The only other name or titles for God used in these books are: Eloah (Hab 1:11; 3:3); "My Holy One" (Hab 1:12; 3:3); "O Rock" (Hab 1:12); and Shepherd (Mic 2:12; 7:14; Zech 9:16; 10:3). Paul Hanson notes that this predominant Old Testament use of the name Yahweh for God reflects an underlying faith in the one God who redeemed his people from bondage in Egypt and gave them the promised land. Hanson says, "The awesome power of Israel's primal encounter was relived in the hearing of the divine name." The name Yahweh stands for grace, glory, righteousness and praise (Exod 34:5-6). Underlying the variety of themes in these seven books is one theme: 'I am Yahweh your God who brought you up from the house of bondage. You shall have no other gods before me.'"[3]

How does one organize and present the biblical themes in these seven books? Do we make a list of various themes, pull out certain passages from each book, and present the material under the heading of these themes? Or do we take each book separately and present the themes in each book? Either way, we run the risk of destroying the meaning of the material by forcing it into our theological mold. We have chosen the latter method. Separate chapters examine each book. Each chapter consists of a brief introduction to the book and a discussion of each of its major themes. Technical questions of date, authorship, transmission of the text, translation, and interpretation have been discussed in my commentary, *Micah-Malachi*, in the Word Biblical Commentary series, Volume 32 (usually identified in this book as WBC 32). The last chapter will summarize the theology of all seven books.

Is there any connection between the name of a prophet and a theme in his book? The name Micah means "who is like thee?" There seems to be a play on that name in Micah 7:18,

> "Who is like thee, pardoning iniquity?" (RSV)

The name Nahum means "Comforter." In Nahum 3:7 the prophet says,

> Wasted in Nineveh, who will bemoan her?
> Whence shall I seek comforters for her? (RSV)

D. L. Petersen says that Haggai's name, "festival," resonates with the issue of the restoration of the cult (worship), and Zechariah's name, "Yahweh remembers," is a conservative name, "evoking a sense of continuity with earlier Israelite tradition. Such a name suggests that Yahweh remembers what he did for and with Israel at an earlier period. And it presumes he will act again in a similar manner."[4]

Although there are obvious connections between the name of a prophet and some aspect of his message, we need to be cautious in using any play on words to discover biblical themes or interpret any passage. We should, however, be sensitive to biblical meanings and methods. Ancient ways of writing and thinking were not always the same as ours. We must listen to the text without forcing it into shapes and molds not inherent to it.

I must express my gratitude and appreciation to John D. W. Watts and the editors of Word Books for the opportunity to contribute this volume to the Word Biblical Themes series. It has been a stimulating and enlightening study. My sincere gratitude goes also to Mrs. Gloria Wells, who has done yeoman's service in the production of this manuscript. My wife of almost forty-five years, Dorothy, has supported and encouraged me all along the way, for which I am very glad.

This small volume is dedicated to our grandsons, Daniel and David Leverenz. I pray that they and every reader will find and appropriate God's love, forgiveness, guidance, and sustenance offered in the pages of these seven prophets.

Ralph L. Smith
Southwestern Baptist Theological Seminary
Fort Worth, Texas

2 THEMES IN MICAH

'Who is like Yahweh? (Micah 7:18)

Introduction

The book of Micah is one of the great books of the Bible. It consists of only seven short chapters. But its power and influence vastly outweigh its size. Although the book has often been ignored or neglected, some of its words are unforgettable. Who can forget, for example, those words of global disarmament and universal peace:

> They [Nations] shall beat their swords into plowshares
> and their spears into pruning hooks.
> Nation shall not lift up sword against nation,
> and they shall not train again for war. (4:3)

The words of Micah are linked inseparably to the Christian faith by his prediction of the birth of a ruler of Israel in Bethlehem-Judah:

But you, Bethlehem Ephrathah,
small among the clans of Judah,
from you shall come forth for me
one to be a ruler in Israel,
whose origin is from of old,
from ancient days. (5:2)

The prediction was fulfilled beyond the prophet's fondest dreams in the birth of Jesus of Nazareth (Matt 2:6). Wherever the gospel is preached, the words of Micah will be remembered.

Micah's summary of God's requirements of man in 6:8 has been praised by great and small alike. Thomas Huxley, (1825–1895) the famous British scientist, called it "a perfect ideal of religion." It has been inscribed in the Library of Congress as a summary of religion. It has been sung in the Sistine Chapel on Good Friday to the music of the sixteenth-century Italian composer Palestina (1526–1594). Artists and painters have portrayed their understanding and impressions of the prophet on paper, canvas, and murals.

In 1890 James Singer Sargent was commissioned to decorate the walls of the great hall in the Boston Public Library. By 1919 he completed "The Frieze of the Prophets" on the north end of the hall. The frieze consists of eighteen mural paintings of the prophets, nine on each side of the central figure of Moses. On the far left are four prophets of despair (Hosea, Obadiah, Joel, and Zephaniah). On the extreme right are four prophets of hope (Micah, Haggai, Malachi, and Zechariah). The last three prophets on the right face the future with a look of hope on their faces. Micah, the fourth from the right end of the frieze, has his head turned away from the light. His left hand covers his eyes as he ponders the wrongdoings of men and nations.

Saul Raskin, a Russian-born American Jew painted the prophet as a farmer lifting his eyes from the field toward

Jerusalem, which to Micah was the center of wealth and power. Behind him in the painting is a slave driver with lash lifted against the unfortunate laborers of the grasping, heartless landlord. Micah stands between the evils in the country-side and the corruption in the city. Behind him shines the rising sun, as bright as the promises at the end of the book.[1]

> He will turn and show us compassion.
> He will tread down our iniquities
> and He will cast all our sins
> into the depths of the sea. (7:19)

Unlike Raskin, Hans Walter Wolff does not see Micah as a farmer. Although a man from the country, Micah is neither a poor peasant nor an agricultural worker. He is a prophet and an elder of Moresheth, like the leaders of Judah, (Jer 26:17; 1 Sam 30:26). Micah knows what an elder has to do in a Judean town—sharing in the judicial process in the gate and, perhaps, imparting clan wisdom. He knows at least three problems which that wisdom speaks against in Proverbs: oppression of free citizens (Mic 2:2; 3:3, 10; Prov 14:13; 22:16); corrupt judging (Mic 3:11; Prov 17:15; 18:5); and undisciplined drinking (Mic 2:11; Prov 20:1; 21:17; 23:20-21). He knows justice and the forms of laments (1:8-16; 2:1). Wolff suggests testing the disputed passages in Micah on the basis of whether they might come from the sphere of an elder in Judah in the last third of the eighth century B.C.[2]

Micah probably was the youngest of the quartet of writing prophets who lived in the last half of the eighth century B.C. The other three were Amos and Hosea in the northern kingdom and Isaiah in the south. Micah's ministry may be dated by the reigns of the three kings of Judah mentioned in the superscription: Jotham (740-735 B.C.), Ahaz (735-715 B.C.), and Hezekiah (715-688 B.C.). Micah probably began his ministry before the fall of Samaria in 722 B.C. because he refers to its coming doom in 1:6-7.

Most of Micah's ministry was spent near the end of the eighth century in Jerusalem, where he may have fled as a refugee from the onslaught of Sennacherib's army against southern Judah. According to Sennacherib's account of that invasion, which took place about 701 B.C., he captured forty-six walled cities and innumerable smaller villages. He says he carried away captive 200,150 people—young and old, male and female—and he also took as spoils of war innumerable horses, mules, donkeys, camels, and cattle. He shut up Hezekiah, king of Judah, like a caged bird within Jerusalem.[3]

Life in Israel and Judah was extremely difficult in those last decades of the eighth century B.C. Assyria ruled with an iron hand. Foreign influences on society and religion were strong. Callused, unscrupulous businessmen in Israel oppressed the poor (2:1-2; 6:10-12). Prophets divined for money and priests taught for hire (3:11). Rulers and judges abhorred justice and asked for bribes (3:6-7; 7:3). People could not trust neighbors or immediate family (7:5). The godly man, it seemed, had perished from the earth (7:2).

Against this historical, social and religious background, we may ask what are the major themes of Micah? We find in his book the two major themes of most Old Testament prophets, judgment and hope. But in a sense Micah had only one topic: "Yahweh is Lord." Micah was intoxicated with the presence and power of God. Other prophets might go about uttering wind and lies, saying,

> I will preach to you of wine and strong drink. (2:11)

Micah said:

> On the other hand I am full of power,
> the spirit of God,

and justice and might,
to tell to Jacob his transgression
and to Israel her sin. (3:8)

Under the umbrella of Micah's theocentric message, we may detect at least three other important themes that answer the question incorporated in the meaning of his name, "Who is like Yahweh?" The three major themes are: (1) Yahweh is a God who speaks; (2) Yahweh is a God of requirements; and (3) Yahweh is a God of redemption, restoration, and hope.

Yahweh is a God who speaks

People in Micah's time were seeking a word from God, but they were seeking it in the wrong place and in the wrong way. They were consulting sorcerers and soothsayers (5:12), diviners and false prophets (3:7), but they were getting no answer from God. Micah said:

> Thus says Yahweh concerning the prophets
> the ones leading my people astray. . . .
> It shall be night to you without vision,
> and darkness to you without divination. . . .
> The seers shall be ashamed,
> and the diviners will be confused,
> and all of them will cover their lip
> because there is no answer from God. (3:5-7)

The message of Micah is clear: people cannot force or manipulate God into speaking. A prophet or soothsayer cannot pry secrets out of God. People do not find God; God finds them. God speaks to people, only on His terms. Sometimes when people speak to God, there is no answer.

> They will cry out to Yahweh,
> but he will not answer them.

But he will hide his face from them
at that time,
according to the wickedness of their deeds. (3:4)

However, Micah is certain that God does speak. He says:
". . . they shall sit every man under his vine and under his
fig tree, and none shall make them afraid; for the mouth of
the Lord of hosts has spoken" (4:4 RSV). Four times in this
book Micah claims to speak for God by using the expression
"Thus says the Lord" (2:3; 3:5; 4:6; 5:20). The book opens
with the assertion that "The word of the Lord came to
Micah of Moresheth" (1:1). The word of God is specific. It
came to or through Micah of Moresheth. It is addressed to
the people of Samaria and Jerusalem (1:1, 6). It identifies
specific sins and sinners. God's Word is also both individual
and universal:

He has declared to you, O man, what is good (6:8).
Hear, you peoples all of you;
Listen, O earth and all her fullness (1:2).

It is difficult to think in global or universal terms. The
human race is so divided and segmented—racially, religiously,
nationally, and geographically—that it is almost impossible to
see the whole world in one broad picture.

Our condition calls to mind the early days of photography,
when large group pictures were made with an oscillating camera. Since the camera lens was not wide enough to take the
whole group's picture at once, the same person could appear
on both ends of the picture by standing on one side of the
group as the camera began and rushing to the other as
the camera swung around. Now, however, we have cameras
mounted on satellites that can photograph the whole earth
from thousands of miles above it

Micah understood that God can see the whole earth and address everything and everyone in it. He believed God not only sees the whole world, but he also controls nature and history, in a purposeful, beneficent sense.

Not only is God's Word in Micah universal, addressing the nations throughout, it is also urgent. Three times the prophet uses the imperative form of the word, "Hear" (1:3; 3:1, 9), and once he uses the word "hearken" in the imperative (1:2).

The urgency of this word strikes us at once. "Hear all you people; hearken, O earth and all that is in it" (RSV). It says, in effect, "Pay attention." Stop what you are doing and listen. Not that this is easy to get people to do. Karl Menninger[4] told of a man standing on a street corner in the Chicago Loop in 1972 pointing at pedestrians as they passed and saying, "Guilty." The effect was almost eerie. People would hesitate, stare at him, then hurry on. People in Micah's time were in a hurry, too. They did not want to be interrupted to listen to someone claiming to have a word from God. But God was in a hurry as well. His word had a note of urgency in it. "Hear, hearken, behold the Lord is coming. . ." (1:3 RSV).

Many who heard Micah tried to silence him. They were satisfied with things as they were. They said to Micah,

> "'Stop preaching,' they preach.
> One (they) must not preach these things.
> Calamity will not overtake us." (2:6)

Micah said on behalf of the Lord,

> And I will make Samaria
> a heap for the field,
> planting places for a vineyard.
> And I will pour out her stones into the valley
> and her foundations I will uncover. (1:6)
> Therefore, on your account Zion

shall become a plowed field
and Jerusalem shall become a ruin,
and the mount of the house
a forest high place. (3:12)

Micah realized the gravity of the situation and he said,

For this I will beat my breast and howl
I will go barefoot and naked.
I will lament like jackals,
and mourn like an ostrich
Because incurable is her wound,
because it has come to Judah
. . . even [to] Jerusalem. (1:8–9)

Micah saw his society as terminally ill. He was ready to dial 911. Are there parallels between Micah's society and ours? Is our society in a state of rigor mortis? Arnold Toynbee once pointed to twenty-one civilizations and noted that the one in which we now live is clearly suffering from most of the ailments that destroyed those that have died. But who among us is beating his breast and howling like a jackal?

The Word of God was specific and clear as to what was wrong with society in Micah's day. At first, Micah used general words for moral evil: "transgression," and "sin" (1:5). Then he identified religious or spiritual evils, pointing to "images," "idols," and "harlotry" as violations of covenant commandments (1:7). He also identified other sins of his people:

- devising wickedness (2:1)
- coveting and seizing fields (2:2)
- oppressing a man and his family (2:2)
- walking haughtily (2:3)
- stripping the robe from the poor (2:8)
- driving women and children off of their land (2:9)

- eating people alive (3:3)
- leaders leading the people astray (3:5)
- committing commercial crimes (6:10–11)
- using violence and lies (6:12)
- committing murder and intrigue. (7:2b)

Micah saw that the wound of such a society was incurable (1:9). He affirmed that his people would experience ruin and despair. But beyond the disaster was the hope and promise of redemption and restoration.

Yahweh is a God of requirements

Someone said that prophetic religion is as hard as it is holy. Micah believed there was a sternness in God's judgment: "[God] will by no means clear the guilty" (Exod 34:7 RSV)

But some people in Micah's day were moral and religious relativists. They said, "'One should not preach of such things; disgrace will not overtake us'" (2:6 RSV). Micah said that they abhorred justice, perverted equity, built Zion with blood, took bribes, divined for money, yet leaned on the Lord and said, "Is not the Lord in the midst of us, no evil shall come upon us" (3:11 RSV). Such people hated good, loved evil, and tore skin and flesh from the bones of the righteous (3:2). For them, there were no absolutes such as good and evil. Whatever they thought was right, was right for them.

But thinking something is right does not make it so. Would a physicist say to a colleague, "We may disagree on the validity of this experiment. What you consider correct is true for you but what I consider correct is true for me?" It is not what one thinks that determines truth in physics. God created man and the universe, and he regulates life and the world with moral and physical laws. Those laws, grounded in the nature of God, determine truth. Truth is one. It is singular. As Harold Bosley said:

15

When the ancient Israelite chanted his Shema, 'Hear, O Israel, the Lord thy God is one Lord,' he was giving the true religious final answer to all forms of relativism whether religious or moral.[5]

Micah's terminology for sin and transgression indicates that God had requirements and the people should have known them. The Hebrew word for "sin," *hata*, means "to miss the mark." There had to be a mark before one could miss it. The word for "transgression" is *pesha* which means "rebellion." *Pesha* is a personal word about a son or a vassal who rebels against his father or his lord. Micah speaks of the Lord God being a witness against the people (1:2). He said to the leaders of Israel, "Is it not for you to know justice? (3:1). The greatest passage concerning God's requirements is in 6:8:

> He has declared to you, O man, what is good.
> and what is Yahweh seeking from you?
> Nothing but to do justice, to love devotion,
> and to walk humbly with your God.

The first word, "declared," is a causative form of a verb expressing completed action. God had told, declared, shown "man" (Adam and all people) what is "good." The Old Testament contains no treatise on the nature of goodness, truth or justice. The people of Israel knew they had been addressed by the Lord (Yahweh). They had been told what was required of them, and what was required of them was good. They were not given ethical abstractions. They knew good is what God requires and evil is what God forbids. It is the will of a particular God (Yahweh), not the gods of the nations, that man has to follow to do that which is good. Several times we read in the Old Testament "God is good" (Ps 100:5; 136:1). God himself is good (Mark 10:18). The good is not a mere attribute of

God; it is part of his essence. The good has no existence outside of God. "What God wills, that is the good."[6]

Micah identified the good with God's requirements. He lists three basic ingredients of the good as three requirements of God: (1) do justly; (2) love devotion; and (3) walk humbly with God. There are three levels of requirements here: (1) outward acts—"do justice," (2) inner resources—"love loyalty," and (3) humble relationship with God.

Justice is the mortar that holds society together. Disraeli said, "Justice is truth in action." Raymond Calkins said, "True religion is something higher than religious observances." It is not sacrificing animals, ourselves or others. It is not a creed to believe, a feeling we experience, or something we cannot do. Justice is fair-mindedness in action. It encompasses every area of life: play and business, capital and labor, buyer and seller. Justice is the badge of character. At home or away, it rules out harsh, unfair treatment of others, fault-finding, and conclusions not founded in fact. One man said that to build on injustice is to build on a time bomb. No permanent social order or lasting organization is built without justice.

But justice alone is not enough. To love mercy, kindness, devotion is a cut above "doing justice." One can "do justice" without love. Loving "kindness" is the child of love. Paul said, "Love suffers long and is kind." Love is a matter of the heart and emotions. Kindness enriches the giver and the receiver.

But kindness and justice are not enough. The basic ingredient of goodness is humility. God seeks us that we may humbly walk with him. "To do justice" means to do what God requires. "To love" means to give where no giving is required. But a humble walk with God is the one necessary ingredient of goodness. It is only then that we will truly "do justice" and "love mercy." It is not in the name of justice, or even mercy, that Micah speaks, but in the name of the one who alone is good (Ps 100:5; 136:1; Mark 10:18). It is only as we walk humbly with him that we approach "goodness."

No one can ever accuse Micah and other classical prophets of being soft on sin, crime, injustice, greed, oppression. No man ever loved his native soil more than Micah. He lamented and wailed like a jackal. He went around Jerusalem naked, or clad in a loin cloth, because of what was happening to his people and his native land (1:8). But he never gave up hope. He said:

> But I will watch for Yahweh,
> I will wait for the God of my salvation,
> my God will hear me. (7:7)

Perhaps no man ever preached a sterner message of merited retribution for flagrant sins than Micah. He accused the wealthy land grabbers of cannibalism. He began his message with an announcement that the Lord himself was coming from his temple to destroy Samaria. He would pour down her stones into the valley and uncover her foundations (1:16). Micah said to his people in Judah,

> Therefore because of your account Zion
> shall become a plowed field;
> and Jerusalem shall become a ruin,
> and the mount of the house
> a forest high place. (3:12)

Micah was sure that judgment was coming. He was frank and fearless in his proclamation of judgment. He told it like it was, without regard for personal consequences. Those who were the target of Micah's condemnation tried to silence him. They said, "Do not preach such things" (2:6). Those people certainly did not invite him to dinner. They did not put food in his mouth so that he would preach what they wanted to hear (3:5). He spoke the message God gave him—regardless of the consequences.

Micah affirms that his people will experience ruin and disaster, but beyond the despair is the prospect of redemption. God's last word is not judgment, but redemption, deliverance, restoration. Micah's harshest word of judgment was the word about Zion being plowed as a field and Jerusalem becoming a heap of ruins. The mountain where the temple stood would become a forest. But that harsh word is followed with a word about that mountain of the house of the Lord being exalted and becoming the highest mountain. All nations would flow into it and be taught the ways of God. Universal peace would reign in the earth (4:2-3).

Three times Micah contrasted the degradation of the "now" generation with what would come after judgment. In 4:9-10 he says, "Now you shall go to Babylon; but from there Yahweh will redeem you from the hand of your enemies." In 4:11-13 they were "now" surrounded by profane nations, but the nations did not know that this was only God's plan to thresh the nations like sheaves on a threshing floor. In 5:1-4 Jerusalem was "now" under siege. The ruler in Jerusalem was weak, suffering humiliation at the hands of foreigners, but a new David would be born in Bethlehem and would deliver his people.

For Micah, the present was under judgment, but he had hope for a new day of redemption. Perhaps he was speaking of himself and his people when he said,

> Do not rejoice over me, my enemy!
> Although I have fallen I will arise.
> Although I sit in darkness
> Yahweh will be light to me.
> The rage of Yahweh I will bear
> because I sinned against him.
> Until he pleads my case

19   Themes in Micah

and brings about my justice.
He will bring me out to the light,
and I will see his righteous. (7:8–9)

Micah looked for the day when the smoke of battle would
clear, and swords would be turned into plowshares, and all
military training camps would be abandoned. He would re-
tire to his boyhood farm to sit under his vine and fig tree.
There would be no reason to fear—no drug traffic, no bank
robbers, no child abusers. All this would be possible because
God would pardon iniquity, and forgive sins. He would have
compassion on his people when they confessed their sins.
He would cast all their sins under his feet and into the
depths of the sea.

Who is God like thee,
the one taking away guilt
and passing over the rebellion
of the remnant of his heritage?
He does not keep his anger strong forever,
for he delights in the steadfast love.
He will turn and show us compassion.
He will tread down our iniquities,
and he will cast all our sins
into the depths of the sea.
You will give truth to Jacob,
steadfast love to Abraham
which you swore to our fathers
from days of old. (7:18–20)

The basic problem of Israel was sin. Only God could deal
with it effectively; and he did, and does, in Christ.

3 THEMES IN NAHUM

"Whence shall I seek comforters for you?" (3:7)

Introduction

Nahum is a short, powerful book. It has only three chapters and forty-seven verses. Yet its opening words take away our breath with talk about Yahweh's jealousy, vengeance, and anger against his enemies (1:2). By his power Yahweh rebukes the sea and dries up rivers. He makes vegetation wither, mountains quake, hills melt; and he lays waste the earth and its inhabitants (1:4-5). This is poetry, but it is terrifyingly vivid poetry.

Nahum's book is a "literary masterpiece."[1] Raymond Calkins called Nahum "the last of the great Hebrew poets."[2] The beauty and vividness of Nahum's language appear in the expression, "The clouds are the dust of his feet" (1:3). The beauty of such language seems inconsistent with the harsh themes of God's wrath against Nineveh. Why did Nahum describe God's wrath and judgment in such graphic style? Perhaps to emphasize the importance of the message: all evil will eventually be destroyed.

The origin and unity of the book of Nahum are matters of much debate. Scholars have tried unsuccessfully to trace the history of its formation for more than a century. The book consists of a number of small units. The first eight verses are a broken acrostic on the nature and sovereignty of God. But neither the form nor the subject of the acrostic continue through the rest of the chapter. Verses 9–14 of chapter 1 address Nineveh. Chapter 2 is a vivid poetic description of the battle for Nineveh, ending in a brief prose oracle of judgment against her (2:13). Chapter 3 has a number of units: a woe oracle or lament (3:1–4), an oracle of judgment on Nineveh (3:5–7), a poetic comparison of the fate of Thebes and Nineveh (3:8–13), and some satirical warnings for Nineveh (3:14–17).

It is not yet possible to determine all the processes that went into the origin, selection, and arrangement of the materials in the book as it stands. Perhaps the book was used at one time in Israel in a religious festival celebrating the fall of her enemies.

Nahum was a prophet who lived in Elkosh (a Galilean town, probably, near present-day Capernaum) in the last half of the seventh century B.C. Although Nahum is not called a prophet, the terms "oracle" and "vision" appear in the superscription (1:1). The inclusion of his book in the prophetical section of the Hebrew canon also indicates he was a prophet.

Assyria was the dominant world power in Nahum's time. She shared world power with Egypt until 663 B.C. Then Ashurbanipal, the king of Assyria, captured the Egyptian capital, Thebes, and Assyria became the sole potentate of the world. Assyria was a cruel, ruthless conqueror. She slew many of her captives. Many of those not killed were abused, robbed, and deported from their homeland.

Ashurbanipal, the last of Assyria's strong conquerors, died

about 627 B.C. Winds of revolution began to blow through the empire. Captive people became restless as their bonds were loosened. In Judah, the young King Josiah started his reform in 621 B.C. after a copy of the law was found in the temple (2 Kings 22:8–17). At first, the prophet Jeremiah supported Josiah and his reform (Jer 11:1–13). But the reform faltered in the face of resistance from some in Judah who had vested interests in the old system. It failed completely when Josiah was killed in 609 B.C.

In this context, the little-known prophet Nahum announced the end of Assyria. His name appears only once in his book—and nowhere else in the Bible—but it is frequently corroborated in Northwest Semitic inscriptions. The name is an intensive form of a word meaning "full of comfort."[3] Nahum's name, "Comfort," is ironic if applied to his message to Assyria, for he says that he could not find any "comforters for her" (3:7 RSV). The book offers comfort for all who suffer abuse, injustice and oppression because its message is that evil is doomed. Assyria might run roughshod over the people of the world, dispossessing them of property, home and freedom (2:9–13; 3:19), but that would not last forever. Evil will be judged. What Assyria did to others would be done to her (2:13).

God did punish Assyria for her injustice and wickedness. The same fate that befell Thebes happened to Nineveh in 612 B.C. It happened to Samaria in 722 B.C. and to Jerusalem in 586 B.C. God is no respecter of persons. Judgment comes on all evildoers.

In a sense, Nahum is a "foreign prophecy," directed toward Nineveh, though it serves as a warning to all nations. Most Old Testament prophetic books contain a series of such prophecies (Amos 1–2; Isa 13–23; Jer 46–51; Obad; Zeph 2:5–15; Zech 9:1–8). These foreign prophecies indicate that Yahweh is sovereign over all nations, and that he will punish them for their wickedness. But he will also forgive

Themes in Nahum

them when they repent (Jon 3:10) and accept them as his people (Isa 19:23-24; Zech 8:22-23).

Nahum, however, offers no hint of forgiveness for Nineveh. Like the prophet Obadiah, who was almost his contemporary, Nahum's message is very short and directed almost exclusively to the destruction of a foreign nation. Assyria was the focus of Nahum's message, and Edom was Obadiah's villain. W. Gladstone Watson said of Obadiah,

> [His] eyes were too full of tears to see, his heart too bitter to feel, that the heathen must be included in God's purposes of mercy, but he did believe that, in spite of all appearances, God is sovereign and ultimately the kingdom must be the Lord's.[4]

Nahum's eyes, like Obadiah's, were also filled with tears, and bitterness was in his heart. He had no compassion for Nineveh, but he did have a firm conviction that God is sovereign over the whole world.

Three basic themes are interrelated in Nahum: (1) the sovereignty of God, (2) the guilt of Nineveh, and (3) the fall of Nineveh.

The sovereignty of God

The first chapter of Nahum is a theological introduction to the Ode of Nahum, expressing profound faith in the rule of God. Tyrants will be overthrown. God may be merciful. He may be patient. He must be just—his sovereignty demands it. The book of Nahum is "a kind of theodicy, a vindication of the providence of God in the light of human evil and cruelty."[5] It expresses the truth that God is the avenger who will make his enemies his footstool. He has power over the forces of nature. He controls the wind and the storm. He makes the mountains quake and rebukes the sea. He raises up nations

(Hab 1:6), uses them as a rod of his anger (Isa 10:5), and cuts them off because of their wickedness (Isa 40:23-24).

Such language may be too strong for some whose idea of God has been nurtured by the gospel of Christ. Christians think and talk about the love of God, and they should. But if they do not also speak of his wrath, anger, or vengeance, their faith may grow thin and flaccid. We need to hear the reverberating words, "Who can stand before his indignation? And who can abide in the fierceness of his anger?" (Nah 1:6 RSV). Nahum knew that "the Lord is good and is a stronghold in the day of trouble, and he knows those who trust in Him" (1:7).

But Nahum also knew that cognizance of God's goodness and peace must be balanced with an understanding of his justice and wrath. Otherwise loose notions of sin and retribution will result. The goodness of God is not always as apparent as his power. In nature and in the orderings of providence, many ugly facts seem to deny God's goodness and peace. But Nahum, in one of Judah's darkest hours, proclaimed the "good news" that God's goodness would triumph over tyranny and evil (1:15).

It is easy to misunderstand God's jealousy, wrath, and vengeance. Many primitive or misguided people live in terror that some capricious act of God may fall upon them. When Nahum spoke about God's jealousy, wrath or vengeance, however, he was not thinking of God as being capricious. The terms used in 1:2 to describe God's moral nature reveal his repugnance toward the sins of greed, oppression, and brutality.

"Jealousy" describes God's zeal to keep his plans from being opposed or frustrated. He is passionately determined that his rule be accepted throughout his realm. His victory will be for those who take refuge in him. The idea of "vengeance" may go back to the old "kinsman redeemer" concept, or it may be related to ideas in the old suzerain treaties. George Mendenhall argued that the word *nāqām* normally translated "vengeance" is not used of blood feuds. Instead it refers to instances in which the valid suzerain exercises his legitimate power either to save or punish, depending on the recipient's relationship to him. The suzerain claims, "Sovereignty is mine" (Deut 32:25; Rom 12:19).[6]

Vengeance in the Old Testament may mean "to punish" or it may mean "to vindicate." In Joshua 10:13, it means punish. It means vindicate in Judges 11:36, 2 Samuel 22:48, Isaiah 61:1-4. In Nahum, it refers to God's ability to punish, based on his nature as a jealous, judging God. He claims dominion over the entire world. Nineveh had come to represent evil opposed to God. He exercised his eternal power and judgment upon her.[7]

According to Nahum, the Lord is patient and judicious in his use of his great power, but he will not clear the guilty (1:3b).

The guilt of Nineveh

God's moral outrage expressed in his jealousy, anger, and vengeance is provoked by Assyria's guilt. Nahum quoted one of Israel's creeds and applied it to Assyria, "The Lord will by no means clear the guilty" (Exod 34:7). What had Assyria done to incur such guilt? First, she had "plotted against the Lord" (1:9) and "counselled villainy" (1:11). The word translated "villainy" or "wickedness" is *beliyya'al* and may mean "those who throw off the yoke of God. People who undermined the monarchy were called "sons of Belial" (1 Sam 10:27; 2 Sam 20:1 KJV). Nahum says the opposition of the king of Assyria to Yahweh is an instrument of evil or chaos (Nah 1:9, 15). One of Assyria's chief sins was a failure to recognize Yahweh's sovereignty. Twice Nahum says on behalf of the Lord, "Behold, I am against you says the Lord of Hosts" (2:13; 3:5). Other prophets also spoke of God's sovereignty over Assyria. Isaiah said,

Ah, Assyria, the rod of my anger,
the staff of my fury!
Against a godless nation I send him,
and against the people of my wrath
I command him
to take spoil and seize plunder,
and to tread them down like the
mire of the streets.
But he does not so intend,
and his mind does not so think;
But it is in his mind to destroy,
and to cut off nations not a few. (Isa 10:5-7 RSV)

Isaiah said that when the Lord finished punishing Judah and Jerusalem, he would punish the arrogant boasting and haughty pride of the king of Assyria (Isa 10:12-19). God would break the power of Assyria and trample him under foot (Isa 14:25; Mic 5:5-6; Zeph 2:13-15). To Yahweh, the king of Assyria was "vile," a light weight. The term "vile" in Nahum 1:14c means "light," "small," "of no significance."

Not only was Assyria guilty because of her plotting against God; she was also guilty because of her rapacious treatment of captives. In the only lament in the book that begins with "woe," Nahum says,

Woe to the city of bloodshed—
full of lies,
full of plunder!
Their prey never ceases. (3:1)

Blood, lies, plunder, harlotries, corpses, filth, and sorceries characterize this passage (3:1-7). Evidently Assyria amassed huge wealth from her conquests. Nahum says,

Themes in Nahum

Plunder silver, plunder gold,
No end to the treasure;
heaps of every precious thing. (2:10)

Isaiah quotes the Assyrian king as saying,

My hand has found like a nest
the wealth of the peoples;
and as men gather eggs that have
been forsaken
so I have gathered all the earth;
and there was none that moved a wing
or opened the mouth, or chirped. (Isa 10:14 RSV)

Nahum compares Assyria's treatment of her captives to a lion carrying captured prey to its mate and cubs in a den filled with mauled, broken carcasses. The New English Bible captures the meaning very well:

The Lion which killed to satisfy its whelps
and for its mate broke the neck of the kill,
mauling its prey to fill its lair,
filling its den with mauled prey. (2:12)

S. R. Driver says that this effective figure of "the ferocity, destructiveness and rapacity displayed by the Assyrians . . . might be illustrated from almost every inscription recording the exploits of the Assyrian kings."[8]

One inscription that illustrates Assyria's ruthlessness comes from the Prisms of Esarhaddon, king of Assyria (680–669 B.C.). In Prism A he says that he hung the heads of two captured kings: "Sandurri, king of Kundi, and Abdim-ilkutte, king of Sidon around the neck of their nobles or chief-officials to demonstrate to the population the power of Ashur, my lord, and parade (thus) through the wide main street of Nineveh with singers (playing on) *sammû*—harps."[9]

Assyria was guilty and Nineveh was about to fall.

The fall of Nineveh

Nineveh was the world's greatest city in her day. In some ways she was alluring and enticing, possessing "graceful and deadly charms" (3:4 RSV). The city was the social and cultural center of the world, a place of magnificent architecture, superior facilities in medicine, science, and literature.[10] But she fell from her highest pinnacle to almost total oblivion in about fifty years (663 to 612 B.C.).

Nineveh fell in 612 B.C. to a coalition of forces from the Medes, Babylonians, and Scythians. Evidently Nahum witnessed the height and eclipse of Assyria's power. It is not necessary to assume Nahum was an eyewitness to the battle for Nineveh. His account of it was probably written slightly before fighting began and in a place far removed from Nineveh itself. No doubt, Nahum had access to other accounts of strategic battles. Here he portrays an oriental siege, with its horrors, cruelties, and savagery, so graphically that the reader can see and feel it. First comes the fighting in the suburbs (2:1). The enemy storms the walls (2:5), then captures the city as its inhabitants try to flee in panic (2:6–8). Finally, the city is torched and the people killed with the sword (3:18). Nahum concludes his work by saying that all who hear the news of Nineveh's fall will celebrate. They will clap their hands—much like the victims of Hitler and Idi Amin did when they heard the news of the tyrants' overthrow.

What are we to make of the message of Nahum that God is a jealous, avenging, and angry God who will not clear the guilty? We need to make allowances for the oriental poetical language and the times and circumstances in which the book is written. We need to remember that Nahum presents two

Themes in Nahum

complementary faces of God: the countenance of a compassionate liberator and an angry face toward those whose oppression makes liberation a constant necessity. Craigie says, "Nahum's is a sturdy theology, not for the weak and squeamish." Liberation involves judgment that "reveals the anger of a righteous God against the ruthlessness of human beings who think they can act with impunity."[11]

Craigie has a timely warning for interpreters of Nahum's message of Nineveh's fall. Nahum was not setting out political theory or trying to enlist recruits against Nineveh. He emphasized that God would act. We are not to thirst to slaughter the enemy in battle so much as we are to seek to transform the evil within ourselves and our society.

For transformation to occur in an individual and/or society three traits of great character must prevail: the capacity for a great love, for a great enthusiasm, and for a great indignation. Nahum had the last of these. The New Testament says, "Be angry and sin not." Being angry is not always a sin. Sometimes it is a sin not to be angry. It is easy to feel superiority to the attitudes reflected in Nahum. But along with love and forgiveness, righteous indignation is sometimes necessary. To neglect the truths underscored by Nahum is to lose a valuable note in the biblical message.

4 THEMES IN HABAKKUK

Behold the soul [of the wicked] is puffed up
and is not upright within him;
but the righteous by his faithfulness
shall live. (2:4)

Introduction

About 609 B.C., Habakkuk followed Nahum as a prophet in Judah. Nahum prophesied that Nineveh would be destroyed and her destruction celebrated universally (Nah 3:19). When Nineveh fell in 612 B.C. there must have been dancing in the streets of Jerusalem because Jerusalem bore the brunt of many of Nineveh's military campaigns. But any such celebration was short-lived because within a few years another terrible tyrant burst on the scene.

In 605 B.C. Nebuchadnezzar, crown prince of Babylon and the leader of her armies, won a decisive victory at Carchemish over Egypt and what was left of Assyria. The battle of Carchemish put an end to the Assyrian empire and ushered in the

Neo-Babylonian period (605–538 B.C.). If Nahum expected a long period of peace to follow the fall of Nineveh, he must have been greatly disappointed. If Habakkuk had high hopes for Judah's restoration and independence after Nineveh fell, his hopes were also dashed rudely to pieces. His own people's wickedness (1:1–4) and the greed and ruthlessness of the Babylonians created serious problems for Habakkuk (1:5–11).

When one tyrannical overlord (Babylon) followed another (Assyria) and Judah herself experienced a moral and religious breakdown, Habakkuk began to ask questions concerning Yahweh's indifference to prayer and his failure to act against evildoers. Yahweh said that he was raising up the Chaldeans, "that bitter and hasty nation" (1:6 KJV, RSV), to bring judgment on Judah. The Chaldeans would run roughshod over the earth and gather captives like sand. They were proud, ruthless, and guilty men (1:5–11).

The Lord's first answer, that he was going to use the terrible Babylonians to punish Judah, created an even greater problem for Habakkuk. Habakkuk asked, how could a holy and everlasting God, whose eyes are too pure to look on evil, use treacherous and wicked men to judge and chasten people more righteous than they? (1:12–17).

Habakkuk's circumstances and experience did not match his theology. He believed that God is good, just, and righteous and that he is also sovereign. The Lord has the whole world in his hands. He controls nations and nature. But if that is true, why is God silent when we pray? Why does he allow evil to go unpunished? How can a righteous God use an evil agent to punish someone more righteous than he? How long will God permit the wicked to swallow the righteous?

> Shall they therefore empty
> their nets, and not spare
> continually to slay the nations? (1:17 RSV)

These were some of the questions Habakkuk was asking as he sought an explanation for why things were happening as they were. He also asked for a time and a date when God would answer all his questions with complete clarity.

At first Habakkuk's questions met only silence. Then he decided to station himself on the tower to see what the Lord would say to him (2:1). Habakkuk wanted to know why the Lord allowed injustice to continue and when he would punish the evildoers. "Why" was Job's question, but the Lord never explained to him why he was suffering. "When" was a question Jesus' disciples asked. Jesus told them that time is the prerogative of God (Acts 1:7). It was not for them to know the day or hour of his coming. Nor did God ever answer Habakkuk's questions of why and when.

God did tell Habakkuk, however, that there was an answer to his question concerning the use of a wicked agent to punish his own people. But the answer was not for Habakkuk alone. It was given for everyone. It was to be written on a tablet in large letters and posted in a prominent place so everyone could read it. The answer took the form of a vision and a promise, revealing something that would happen at a future "appointed time" (2:3). Although the promise was given to Habakkuk, it would not become a reality until later. But the date for its fulfillment had already been set, and "it would surely come" (2:3).

The expression in Hebrew, "it will surely come," is an infinitive absolute before an imperfect verb form. As such it is the strongest possible way to express certainty in Hebrew. The time of the fulfillment was not revealed to Habakkuk and his associates, but it was known to God. From a human vantage point it would tarry, but Habakkuk and his people were to wait expectantly. They were to be busy, however, and not to wait with bated breath and folded hands. People are often overly concerned with God's timetable and with what others might do. On one occasion Peter asked Jesus what would

Themes in Habakkuk

happen to John. Jesus said to Peter, "If it is my will that he remain until I come, what is that to you? Follow me" (John 21:21-22).

The answer the Lord gave Habakkuk to write on the huge tablet that day is "one of the great verses of the Bible."[1]

> Behold, he whose soul is not upright in him shall fail,
> but the righteous shall live by his faith. (2:4 RSV)

This verse is not only great because of the truth it expresses, but also because of the ever-widening influence of the idea of "salvation by grace" hidden in it. F. W. Farrar[2] said that this text has in it a moral steadfastness, a deep trust in God and loyal allegiance to him. Its principle of "justification by faith," enunciated by a seer of whom we know hardly anything beyond his name, is one of the great links connecting all that is spiritual and permanent in the Old and New Testaments.

The Talmud did not overlook the significance of this verse in Habakkuk. According to it, the rabbis had multiplied the laws of Moses into 613 precepts, but David reduced them to 11 (Ps 15); Isaiah to 6 (Isa 33:15); Micah to 3 (Mic 6:8); and Amos to 1, "seek me and live (5:4). This one necessary precept from Amos was set out still more clearly by Habakkuk in the verse, "The just shall live by faith." Farrar said,

> It is no small glory to this prophet that he should have been commissioned to enunciate a message which sums up with such emphatic brevity, yet with such far-reaching fullness, alike the commands and the promises of the Old and New Testaments.[3]

Jesus did not refer to Habakkuk 2:4 in summing up the gospel, but Paul made it the keynote of his theology. He quoted part of the verse in Romans 1:17 and Galatians 3:12 to support his doctrine of salvation by grace. The writer of Hebrews used the Septuagint version of this verse to point out his reader's need of endurance and the fact that they should not "shrink back" (Heb 10:36–39). This verse "became the rallying cry of both Lutheran and Reformed theology."[4] It is the key to the whole of Habakkuk. It does not furnish us intellectual or theological explanations for the problem of evil. It supplies an existential answer. It says that evil is doomed, and the righteous will live by relying on God's promises. It indicates two ways to live: the way of the wicked, which leads to death, and the way of the righteous, which leads to life. The way to life and victory is the way of faith and commitment to God. Three major themes in the book of Habakkuk relate closely to this verse: (1) Evil is doomed, (2) the righteous shall live, and (3) faith is the victory.

Evil is doomed

Habakkuk complains in his first paragraph about the overwhelming presence and power of evil in his society. Evil was everywhere: in the streets, in homes, businesses, governments, and among the nations. It seemed to Habakkuk that little was being done or could be done to stem the tide of evil in his day. The law was frozen, and justice never went forth victorious (1:4). Yahweh did not seem to listen to any prayer or do anything to save his people from violence and injustice (1:2–3).

Habakkuk complained that his own people were committing crimes against each other, and Babylon, a cruel godless invader, was destroying them, too. To make himself rich, the invader treated captives like fish in a net and slaughtered nations without pity (1:14–17). But Habakkuk believed also that Babylon represented a cosmic evil which threatened God and his king. In chapter 3:8–15 Habakkuk spoke of a battle between Yahweh and the rivers, the sea, and the waters, using

Themes in Habakkuk

metaphors from the Exodus and the crossing of the Red Sea. Old mythological language of a battle with the dragon Tiamat is evident in 3:8-15.

The idea that waters symbolized cosmic evil was fairly common in the ancient Near East. A number of Old Testament passages portray Yahweh fighting against evil represented as waters. Unlike some ancient peoples, such as the Phoenicians or the Greeks, the Israelites were more at home with the desert than with the sea. When Habakkuk spoke about God's wrath against the rivers and indignation against the sea (3:8), he was using the same kind of language found in some of the Psalms, Job and Isaiah. Waters are personified as Rahab, Leviathan, Tanin or dragon (Isa 27:1; 51:9-10; Job 3:8; 7:12; 9:13; 26:12). Psalm 93:3-4 says that the floods have lifted up their voices in rebellion against Yahweh. But God is mightier than the thunder of many waters, mightier than the waves of the sea. Job 26:12-13 says:

> By his power he stilled the sea;
> by his understanding he smote Rahab
> By his wind the heavens were made fair;
> his hand pierced the fleeing serpent. (RSV)

Psalm 65:6 says that God stills the seas and the roaring of their waves. In Psalm 69:1-2, 14 the psalmist compares his enemies to water:

> Save me, O God!
> For, the waters have come up to my neck.
> I sink in deep mire,
> where there is no foothold;
> I have come into deep waters,
> and the flood sweeps over me.
> With thy faithful help rescue me
> from sinking in the mire;

let me be delivered from my enemies
and from the deep waters. (RSV)

Another psalmist compares his strong enemy to many
waters:

He reached from on high, he took me,
he drew me out of many waters.
He delivered me from my strong enemy,
and from those who hated me;
for they were too mighty for me. (Ps 18:16-17 RSV)

Habakkuk knew the power of evil was like a monster, like
many waters. Such powers were too mighty for him and his
people, but God was sovereign over the sea. When the apostle John lived in exile on Patmos, he looked for a day when
there would be "no more sea"—meaning "no more evil" (Rev
21:1). Revelation 12:7-12 reveals God to be as sovereign over
evil as he is over the sea. It speaks about a war in heaven
between Michael and his angels and the dragon and his angels. The dragon and his angels are defeated and cast out of
heaven. The victory is attributed to the blood of Christ and
the faithful witness of Christian martyrs (Rev 12:11).

Habakkuk learned not only that evil is doomed but also
that character alone abides. "Tyranny (evil) is suicide,"[5] and
"he whose soul is puffed up within him shall fail" (2:4a RSV).
The message of the five woes, which follows this verse, is
essentially the same as that of 2:4. The haughty, dis-
honest thief and exploiter mentioned in the five woes is
doomed. It sometimes seems that the power structures of
this world are in the hands of the wicked, but God is still on
the throne. James Russell Lowell wrote:

Careless seems the great Avenger;
history's pages but record

Themes in Habakkuk

One death-grapple in the darkness
twix old systems and the Word;
Truth forever on the scaffold,
wrong forever on the throne—
Yet that scaffold sways the future, and,
behind the dim unknown,
standeth God within the shadow,
keeping watch above his own.[6]

D. Martyn Lloyd Jones said that the five woes in chapter 2 of Habakkuk illustrate a universal principle of history: "Everything that is evil is under the judgment of God."[7] John Paterson noted that Habakkuk expresses his belief in the "ultimate decency of things."[8] That may not be evident over a short period of time, but in the long run it is true. Paterson observed that Nero may sit in his chariot as it clatters up Capitol Hill in Rome and Paul may languish in a Roman jail. But a day comes when people call their children "Paul" and their dogs "Nero." We need to take the long look and ask what the centuries say against the hours. They say, "Evil is doomed; the righteous shall live by faith."

The righteous shall live

If the wicked are doomed and have no future, the other side of the coin is that the righteous shall live. Who are the righteous, and what does it mean "to live?" The term "righteous" has more than one meaning in the Old Testament. In Psalm 1, the righteous are those who shun all forms of evil and folly, and meditate on the law of the Lord day and night. In Proverbs, the righteous are the "wise" ones contrasted against the foolish wicked (Prov 11:5–12). Sometimes Scripture gives checklists for those who would enter the temple to determine if a person is righteous. Such lists may be found in Ps 5, 15, 24; Isa 33:14-15. Ezekiel 18:5-9 gives one definition of a righteous man:

> If a man is righteous and does what
> is lawful and right—if he does not
> eat upon the mountains or lift up his
> eyes to the idols of the house of Israel,
> does not defile his neighbor's wife or
> approach a woman in her time of impurity,
> does not oppress anyone, but restores
> to the debtor his pledge, commits no
> robbery, gives his bread to the hungry
> and covers the naked with a garment,
> does not lend at interest or take any
> increase, withholds his hand from iniquity,
> executes true justice between man and man,
> walks in my statutes, and is careful to
> observe my ordinances—he is righteous,
> he shall surely live, says the Lord God. (RSV)

There you have it, one definition of a righteous man. But are there other ways a person might be considered righteous in the Old Testament? Most Old Testament theologians agree that "righteousness" in the Old Testament means "conformity to a norm"—the covenant relationship between God and man.

Habakkuk uses the term "righteous" three times (1:4, 13; 2:4). In 1:4 and 13, the term is used in contrast to the "wicked" (a term which might have been in the original form of the text in 2:4). These verses define the righteous negatively: he is the victim of his country's ruthless invader and of such social evils as violence, destruction, strife, and contention. But 2:4 attaches a slightly different meaning to the righteous than 1:4 and 13. In 2:4, the "righteous" is not puffed up. He is "right" on the inside, and is committed to serving the Lord faithfully, regardless of times and circumstances.

The apostle Paul and Martin Luther saw this kind of righteousness as the kind that comes by faith. Habakkuk came very close to the idea expressed in Genesis 15:6. God promised Abraham a great posterity, and even though Abraham and his wife were very old and the prospects for the fulfillment of the promise were almost nil, Abraham "believed God and he reckoned it to him as righteousness" (RSV). Perhaps the translators of the Septuagint, and certainly the apostle Paul, saw in Habakkuk 2:4 the idea of "salvation by faith."

Faith is the victory

Contrary to a popular legend, Martin Luther did not say, after he climbed the twenty-eight steps in front of the Lateran church and palace in Rome in 1510, "The just shall live by faith." He said, "Who knows whether it is so?"[9] Luther went to Rome searching for ways to attain peace with God. He spent a month saying confession, celebrating Mass at sacred shrines, visiting catacombs and basilicas, venerating bones and holy relics. He was greatly disillusioned by much that he experienced in Rome, and he did not find peace there. Luther commented that he went to Rome "with onions and returned with garlic." It was not until Luther assumed the chair of Bible at the University of Wittenberg and began exegeting and teaching the Scriptures that he found peace with God. He said that he greatly longed to understand Paul's Epistle to the Romans. What stood in the way was that one expression, "the justice of God." He took it to mean that God is just and deals justly in punishing the unjust. Although he was an impeccable monk, Luther stood before God as a sinner with a troubled conscience and no confidence that his merit would assuage God. He says:

Night and day I pondered until I saw the connection between the justice of God and the statement that 'the just shall live by his faith.' Then I grasped that the justice of God is that righteousness by which through grace and sheer mercy God justifies us through faith. Thereupon I felt myself to be reborn and to have gone through open doors into paradise.[10]

Luther's translation of Habakkuk 2:4 in the German Bible reflects his personal experience.

> Behold he who is stiff-necked (obstinate),
> shall have no rest (*Ruhe*) in his heart,
> but the righteous shall live by his faith.

Luther found rest, joy, and victory when he understood that justification was a gift from God and not the result of his merit or merits from saints.

Habakkuk was not talking about personal salvation in his day. His problem was the wicked tyrant Babylon and the social and religious evils of his own people. He remembered earlier days when the great saving acts of God delivered Israel from Egypt. He had heard how Yahweh came from Teman to subdue the enemies of God's people (3:3-15). Now he wanted God to do it again. He knew he was powerless to correct all the evils in society, but he believed that God could and would save his people.

> I have heard and my belly quakes,
> my lips quiver at the sound,
> rottenness comes into my bones,
> my steps tremble under me.
> I will wait calmly for the day of distress
> to come upon the people attacking us. (3:16)

Themes in Habakkuk

Somewhere in the last section of Habakkuk (3:16–19) the prophet's fear changed to faith, and the change probably comes in 3:16c.[11] Habakkuk was frightened when he thought of the coming of the Babylonians and when he remembered God's rescue of Israel at the Red Sea. But he knew that "joy in the Lord" does not depend on outward circumstances.

> If the fig tree does not blossom,
> and no fruit is on the vines;
> the labor of the olive fails,
> and the fields make no food;
> and the flock is cut off from the pen,
> and no ox is in the stall;
> yet I will exult (cohortative)[12] in Yahweh
> I will rejoice (cohortative) in the God
> of my salvation! (3:17–18)

According to Donald Gowan,[13] Habakkuk was saying "Even though I starve to death, yet I will rejoice in the Lord." Gowan said these words haunted him more than any other in the Bible. He thought of putting them on the wall of his study, but that was not where they belonged. They belong inside a person as one's entire orientation to life. These verses make clear what it means to live by faith. It means to go on doing the right thing, regardless of what happens. Material blessing may or may not come to the righteous, but true rest and joy will come to the person who waits in faith on the Lord. Faith is the victory!

5 THEMES IN ZEPHANIAH

Seek Yahweh, all you humble
of the earth,
who carry out his ordinances.
Seek righteousness, seek humility.
Perhaps you may be hidden
in the day of Yahweh's wrath. (2:3)

Introduction

If the book of Habakkuk relates closely to the Protestant Reformation and to Paul's letters to the Romans and the Galatians, Zephaniah's book might be linked to the Roman Catholic tradition. The medieval hymn *Dies irae, dies illa* "Day of wrath, that day" is based on parts of the book of Zephaniah. The title *Dies irae, dies illa* also comprises the first four words of Jerome's translation of Zephaniah 1:15 in the Latin Vulgate.

This unique hymn was probably written by Thomas of Celano, a companion of Francis of Assisi, about 1255. In

Latin, it consists of seventeen three-line stanzas. The first six stanzas give an awe-inspiring description of Judgment Day. The rest of the hymn consists mainly of deeply personal pleadings for forgiveness and salvation. Originally this sequence or requiem was used as an Advent hymn. Soon it became a part of the Italian missals used as a requiem in the Mass for the dead and as a sequence for All Souls' Day.[1] *Dies irae* became part of the Tridentine Missal at the Council of Trent, and its use in the requiem Mass for the dead became mandatory.[2] Wherever the requiem Mass for the dead has been said since 1563 (Council of Trent), the Book of Zephaniah has been quoted.

But the use of *Dies irae* has not been limited to those in the Roman Catholic tradition. It has been translated into many languages and has appeared in many Protestant hymnals. It has been set to music by such great composers as Mozart and Verdi. It profoundly influenced the writings of men like Sir Walter Scott and Goethe. It furnished the grand climax to Scott's *Lay of the Last Minstrel* (1805). Lockhart, Scott's biographer, said that Scott murmured its lines as he lay dying. Goethe used *Dies irae* effectively in his well-known work, *Faust*. Philip Schaff called it the greatest hymn in the world. Peter Craigie says that the hymn continues to speak to us both as a reflection on the Judgment Day and as a prayer for mercy.[3]

We know very little about the man whose words inspired this great hymn. Zephaniah's name probably means "Yahweh hides"—perhaps emblematic of the terrible days of the reign of Manasseh (688–642 B.C.). The writer of Kings says the evil that Manasseh did in the sight of the Lord was like the abominable practices of the surrounding nations. He rebuilt the high places, erected altars to Baal and the Asherah, and worshiped the hosts of heaven. He burned his son as an offering and practiced soothsaying and augury (2 Kings 21:2-6). He shed much innocent blood, filling Jerusalem from one end to the other (2 Kings 21:16). That was the situation when Zephaniah was born.

The superscription to Zephaniah's book (1:1) traces his genealogy back four generations to a certain Hezekiah. Although many assume this refers to King Hezekiah (the father of Manasseh, who reigned in Jerusalem from 715 to 688 B.C.), we cannot be sure it is the same person. Hezekiah was a common name in Judah (1 Chr 3:23; Ezra 2:16; Neh 7:21), so this Hezekiah could have been someone other than the king. According to 2 Kings 21-22 there were only two generations between Hezekiah and Josiah, not three as the superscription suggests. Also, Amariah is not attested as one of Hezekiah's sons. The social and religious conditions reflected in the book, however, fit into the period of Manasseh and the early part of Josiah's reign. Zephaniah prophesied during the reign of Josiah (640-609 B.C.), according to the superscription.

The southern kingdom of Judah survived the Assyrian onslaught that destroyed the northern kingdom of Samaria in 722 B.C. But Judah became a vassal state of Assyria. Judah's kings—Ahaz, Hezekiah, Manasseh, Amon, and Josiah—were little more than puppets of Nineveh. A century of subjugation took its toll on the lives of the people of Judah. A lack of economic and religious freedom brought an incursion of foreign influences, rites, and customs. Assyria's influence was stifling, debilitating, degrading, and corrupting. All kinds of idolatry were practiced in Jerusalem (Zeph 1:4, 5). There was an aping of foreign dress, customs, and superstitions (1:6). Violence and fraud were common (1:9). Foreign traders took over the markets (1:10-11). Many were "thickened on their lees" (RSV, a phrase describing the collection of the dregs in the bottom of a wine barrel after years of fermentation)— they refused to do anything. They said in their hearts, "Yahweh will not do good or evil" (1:12). Judah was a shameless nation (2:11), haughty and rebellious (3:1-2). Her leaders were vultures—wanton, profane, faithless men (3:3-4, 7, 11).

In 621 B.C., Josiah began his reform by cleansing the temple. He removed the vessels made for the worship of Baal, Asherah, and the hosts of heaven (2 Kings 23:4). He broke down the houses of the male cult prostitutes (2 Kings 23:7). He removed the horses dedicated to the sun and burned the chariots of the sun with fire (2 Kings 23:11). He pulled down the altars on the roof of the upper chamber of Ahaz (2 Kings 23:12) and put away the mediums, wizards, teraphim, and idols of the nations (2 Kings 23:24). But all of Josiah's good works were not enough to turn the Lord from his great wrath (2 Kings 23:26). No wonder Zephaniah was inspired to announce the Day of the Lord was drawing near—*Dies irae, dies illa*.

Although the Day of the Lord is a major theme of Zephaniah, we must consider some preliminary questions before pursuing it further. One question concerns the position of the book among the twelve minor prophets. Most scholars agree that Zephaniah precedes Nahum and Habakkuk chronologically. Nahum probably preached close to the time of the fall of Nineveh (612 B.C.), and Habakkuk must have preached just before the rise of the Babylonians and the battle of Carchemish (605 B.C.). But Zephaniah seems to address the situation in Jerusalem immediately before Josiah's reform in 621 B.C. If Zephaniah preceded Nahum and Habakkuk, why does his book follow theirs in the canonical order?

A simple answer would be that the books of the Bible are not arranged in strict chronological order. The four Gospels are not arranged chronologically. Hosea was not the first of the minor prophets. That distinction goes to Amos. Length and catchwords, however, may have been factors in arranging some books in the Bible. Hosea may come before Amos because it is longer. Joel may come before Amos because of the catchwords "The Lord roars from Zion" (Joel 3:16 and Amos 1:2 RSV) and "the mountains shall drop down sweet wine" (Joel 3:18 and Amos 9:13 KJV).

Similarly, Zephaniah might have been placed after Habakkuk because of the catchword, "hush" or "be silent" in Habakkuk 2:20 and Zephaniah 1:6. Zephaniah probably was placed before Haggai because the word "time" occurs in Zephaniah 3:20 and Haggai 1:2. Of course, factors other than length of the book and catchwords must be considered before any final conclusion can be reached concerning the arrangement of books in the Old Testament.

Another preliminary question comes from the fact that the book of Zephaniah is neither well-known nor well-liked. It has a somber tone, and the note of judgment is seldom welcomed. Perhaps Zephaniah has an inordinate emphasis on wrath and judgment. It is easy for moderns to dismiss Zephaniah's message as one addressed to an earlier time and of little relevance to the present.

But such an attitude is very unrealistic. The judgment of God is as real today as it was for Zephaniah's age. Judgment was not Zephaniah's only theme, nor is it God's last word. Joy, rejoicing, and hope follow judgment. Although judgment comes on Israel and the nations, a remnant will survive. The nations will be converted (3:9-10).

A tinge of apocalyptic style appears in Zephaniah. His vision is universal. God will come in judgment on the world (3:8). Then there will be a new day. There will be a new unity, a new humility, a new purity, and a new security. There will be no more shame or sinning, no more lies and deceit, no more fear or reproach. The Lord himself will "restore the fortunes of his people" (2:7; 3:20).

In the past, many Old Testament scholars denied that Zephaniah wrote these passages of hope. The same prophet, they said, could not preach judgment and hope at the same time. Few scholars hold such views today, however.

In addition to questions of position and authorship, questions of date arise. John D. W. Watts says, "It is possible that Zephaniah planned the entire prophecy for presentation in temple services within the decade before Josiah's reform in 626 B.C."[4] Many still feel, however, that the book was not completed until the postexilic period.

What are the major themes in Zephaniah? First, we should observe that the book is a theocentric one. The name Yahweh occurs thirty-four times in its fifty-three verses. Zephaniah's name occurs once, and that in the superscription. The word "day," referring to some future time, occurs eighteen times in this book. The major themes must, therefore, revolve around the idea of the "Day of the Lord." Four themes are prominent in this book: a day of wrath, a day of worship, a day of decision, and a new day.

A day of wrath

Habakkuk began his book with a complaint that God would not act against evil (Hab 1:2, 4); Zephaniah begins his with a warning that the whole world is on fire. He says God will sweep away everything: man, beasts, birds, fish. The inhabitants of Jerusalem, the remnant of Baal, idolatrous priests, astrologists, and apostates will all experience judgment. The expression "day of wrath" occurs three times in the book (1:15, 18, 2:2). Other graphic terms used to describe the Day of the Lord include: "bitter," "distress and anguish," "ruin and devastation," "darkness and gloom," "clouds and thick darkness," "trumpet blast and battle cry." The Lord says he will "punish" offenders (1:8-9). The fire of his jealous wrath will suddenly consume all the earth's inhabitants (1:18; 3:3).

We do not know what triggered Zephaniah's announcement of a sudden, cataclysmic world judgment. He gives no account of his call or the occasion of his message. It might have been a visit to the temple, with its hideous idols and pagan rituals, on a festival day. It might have been a trip to the market, with its feverish search for profit. It might have been an invasion by the Scythians, a horde of ruthless tribesmen from the north. It might have been the death of Assyria's King Ashurbanipal in 627 B.C.

Whatever the cause, it was the Lord who determined the time and content of Zephaniah's message. Was Zephaniah's message new? Did it startle many of his hearers? Possibly. The book, with its idea that a day of wrath awaits every human being, is shocking to the careful reader today. If Zephaniah stood at the gate of the temple to deliver his message to the worshipers, as Jeremiah did, his message probably was a surprise and shock to many. If Zephaniah was a prophet who worked closely with temple worship he might have incorporated some old, familiar prophetic traditions into his book to use in the temple celebration of the Royal-Zion festival (a part of the fall festival, celebrating God's election of David and Zion).

A day of worship

Worship seems to be universal, and it is a major theme of Zephaniah. The book begins with an announcement that God is going to sweep away everything from the earth, much as he did with the flood in the time of Noah. This threatened judgment would come not because the people were not worshiping but because their worship was unacceptable. Some people were worshiping Baal. Some had turned to astrology. Some had become syncretistic in their worship, trying to combine faith in God with adherence to pagan religious practices. Others turned their backs from following the Lord and did not seek him or inquire of him (1:6).

Zephaniah (1:7), like Habakkuk (2:20) and Zechariah (2:13), issues a call to worship,

> Be silent before the Lord God!
> Because the day of Yahweh is near,

because Yahweh has prepared a sacrifice.
He has sanctified his guests. (1:7)

Worship calls for a period of quiet reverence before the Lord. The worshiper is to acknowledge God's holiness and sovereignty. Although the worshiper usually brought his own sacrifice, this passage reverses the order: the Lord himself would furnish the sacrifice and sanctify his guests. The false worshipers in Judah would be the sacrifice, along with their possessions (1:8-13). Here was an indictment of Judah's present worshipers. They were preoccupied with activities offensive to God's holiness in the marketplaces, in government halls, and in the temple (1:7-13).

In the Day of the Lord, the blood of the people, like the blood of sacrificial animals, will be poured out as dust and their flesh will be of no more value than the cow chips around the temple (1:17). Their silver and gold will not be able to buy deliverance (1:18).

A glimmer of hope comes in 2:1-3. Zephaniah calls for a religious assembly to seek the Lord and to seek righteousness (2:1-3). Only the humble of the land are invited to worship. The prophet offers no guarantee that the worshipers will be spared: All he can promise is that "perhaps" the humble may be "hidden" in the day of wrath.

This day of judgment will come on all men (Heb. *adam*, 1:17) because they have sinned against Yahweh. The human race as a whole has undermined and polluted the very reasons for its being. A sense of the heavy cloud of God's wrath hangs over our world. We continue to live, but only because of God's grace.

Peter Craigie said that Zephaniah's picture of the situation was that the cosmos was out of control and the earth was "tumbling helter-skelter to its doom."[5] At times our world seems to be out of control, tumbling like a renegade satellite to its fiery end. Man's actions may cause the cosmos to be out of control, but he cannot put it back on track by himself. Only God can do that.

Another significant passage about worship is in Zephaniah 2:11.

> Yahweh will come upon them with terror
> because He famished all the
> gods of the earth;
> and each will worship him
> from his place among the islands of the nations.

Some ambiguity exists as to the precise meaning of this verse. It stands between the oracle of judgment on Moab and Ammon (2:5–10) and the oracle against Ethiopia (2:12). It may be a part of the former oracle, but it may stand alone as a general statement about a time when all nations shall worship Yahweh. They will do so because all of their gods have starved to death from inadequate sacrifices. If this is a separate verse, predicting a time when all the nations of the earth will bow in worship before the Lord, it is a step beyond Isaiah 2:1–4 and Micah 4:1–5, passages which see the nations coming to Jerusalem to worship. Zephaniah anticipates the nations worshiping the Lord in their own lands (see Isa 45:23; Mal 1:11; John 4:23).

Zephaniah does, however, charge Jerusalem with its own failure to worship.

> She obeys no voice;
> she accepts no discipline;
> she does not trust Yahweh
> nor come near her God. (3:2)

This distance and rebellion is surprising because of the kind of God Yahweh is, according to Zephaniah. The Lord is righteous and does no wrong (3:5). The Lord is reliable. Morning by morning, he gives his judgment; at the sunrise he does not fail (3:5). The Lord is ruler: "The King of Israel, the Lord, is in your midst" (3:15 RSV). The Lord is a loving God. According to Zephaniah 3:17, "The Lord will rest in his love for his people" (MT) or he will "renew them" in his love (LXX, RSV)

Zephaniah offers several elements of proper worship. One is "drawing near to God" (3:2 RSV). Others are prayer (3:9) service (3:9), praise (3:14), and a humble, confident trust in God (3:2, 11-12). Worship is a strong theme in Zephaniah False worship can lead to the day of God's judgment; true worship may help one survive such a catastrophe (2:3). Pure worship will characterize the lives of those who participate in the eschaton with God (3:9).

A day of decision

The Day of the Lord will be a day of decision. The very time and circumstances of the day depend solely upon God's choice.

> Because it is my decision to gather nations,
> to collect kingdoms,
> to pour out upon them my fierce anger,
> all the heat of my anger,
> because with fire of my jealousy
> all the earth shall be devoured. (3:8)

The term "my decision" is legal language, mišpāṭî in Hebrew. It is the expression of a judge who has made a decision and has the power and authority to execute it. Some translations include: "my determination is" (KJV, ASV); "my decision is" (RSV); "I have decided" (NIV); "I have made up my mind" (TEV); "I am determined (JB); and "for mine it is" (NEB). The point is that God has decided on a day to judge the nations. Man was not consulted and had no part in the decision-making. A similar view of God's judgment on the nations is described in Joel 3:12–15.

> Let the nations bestir themselves,
> and come up to the valley of Jehoshaphat;
> for there I will sit to judge
> all the nations round about.
> Put in the sickle, for the harvest is ripe.
> Go in, tread, for the wine press is full.
> The vats overflow, for their wickedness is great.
> multitudes, multitudes in the valley of decision!
> for the Day of the Lord is near
> in the valley of decision.
> The sun and the moon are darkened
> and the stars withdraw their shining. (RSV)

In the Old Testament, time and space are interrelated. But space is not in control of time. God is. Space is part of creation. Time did not depend on the creation of the heavenly bodies: they were not created until the fourth day after time began. There is a vast difference between Israel's view of the sun, moon, and stars and that of her neighbors. Writes James Muilenberg,

> [In Israel] the mystery and meaning of time is not resolved by appeal to the cosmic world of space; among the other nations the heavenly bodies are deified and *chronos* spatializes time into extension and duration. In the one, time is grasped in terms of purpose, will, and decision; in the other . . . 'by those who gaze at the stars, who at the new moon predict what shall befall you' (Isa 47:13).[6]

In the Bible, God is in control of time. The great events of holy history are his decision: Creation, the Exodus, the birth of Christ (Gal 4:4), Pentecost, and the coming of the Holy Spirit (Acts 2:1). Israel did not know the way of her history; only God knew it.

Man lives from the day of his birth until the day of his death not knowing what a day will bring. He can say, "This is the day which the Lord has made" (Ps 118:24 RSV). He knows, too, that a decisive, final day is coming. The Lord of hosts has a day when Israel and the nations will be held accountable for the days allotted to them (Isa 2:6–22; Amos 1:3, 6, 9, 11, 13).

The psalmist cried, "My times are in your hands" to express the fact that man's time is God's time (Ps 31:15). Habakkuk spoke of a day when the answer to his question would be verified. God had it on his schedule, though Habakkuk did not know when. God was in charge of time for Zephaniah, too. He said, "At that time I will search Jerusalem with lamps, and punish the men who are thickening upon their lees" (1:12 RSV): "At that time I will change the speech of the nations into a pure speech" (3:9). "Behold, at that time I will deal with all of your oppressors" (3:19 RSV), and "At that time I will bring you home" (3:20 RSV).

A new day

Although the word *new* does not actually occur in Zephaniah the concept is there. The idea of change is expressed in 3:9. The eschaton is often described in terms of something "new." The psalmist and the prophets speak about a "new song" (Ps 96:1; 98:1; Isa 42:10). Prophets wrote that God would do "a new thing" (Isa 42:9; 43:19; 48:6; Jer 31:22); he would create a new heaven and a new earth (Isa 65:17; 66:22); he would make a new covenant with his people (Jer 31:31). He would give them a new name (Isa 62:2), give them a new heart (Ezek 18:31; 36:26), and put a new spirit within them (Ezek 11:19).

Zephaniah said that in "time," that is, in the eschaton, God would give his people a new speech and a new unity (3:9), a new humility (3:11-12), a new purity (3:13a), and a new security (3:13b). In turn, the people of God would have a new song (3:14), a new king (3:15), a renewal of God's love (3:17), a new name (3:19), and a renewal of an old promise (3:20). There is a reference to the promise to Abraham (Gen 12:1-3) in the terms, "name" and "home" as there was at the end of Micah (Mic 7:20) When would all of this happen? Only God knows. Time is in his hand.

6   THEMES IN HAGGAI

> Yet once more, in a little while, I will
> shake the heavens and the earth, the sea
> and the dry land. And I will shake all
> nations, and the desirable things of all
> nations shall come, and I will fill this
> house with glory, says Yahweh of hosts. (2:6–7)

Introduction

The modern traveler in England, sooner or later, will probably visit Coventry Cathedral. The cathedral church of St. Michael was bombed and burned in November 1940 during the first Nazi air raid against Coventry. All that remained of the fifteenth-century church was the 300-foot spire and some of the outside walls. For two decades, the charred hull of that famous church stood as a grim reminder of the ravages of war. By 1962, the people of Coventry, helped by millions of people around the world, built and consecrated a new cathedral. But they left the ruins of the old cathedral side by side with the new one.

In 586 B.C., the temple in Jerusalem was "bombed" and burned by Nebuchadnezzar, king of Babylon. The people of Jerusalem must have felt the same shock and anger over the destruction of their temple by the Babylonians as the people of Coventry did over the destruction of their cathedral by the Nazis. Both communities rallied and rebuilt their worship centers amid controversy. Both groups recognized that the mere reconstruction of a building was not enough. They knew that God's spirit must consecrate the "house" and the people alike, otherwise they would build in vain (Hag 2:5, Ps 127:1)[1]

The person primarily responsible for the rebuilding of the temple in Jerusalem was the prophet Haggai. We do not know much about Haggai. We do not know whether he witnessed the destruction of the first temple. Nor do we know whether he had been a captive in Babylon. Haggai suddenly comes on the scene in Jerusalem in the fall of 520 B.C., preaching the urgency and necessity of rebuilding the temple.

The temple had been in ruins almost seventy years since its destruction by Nebuchadnezzar in 587 B.C. (2 Kings 25:8-9, 13-17; Jer 39:1-3; 52:3-13). Many people in Jerusalem were carried captive to Babylon when Jerusalem fell. Some of those left behind during the time the temple was in ruins probably continued to worship Yahweh at a makeshift altar near the temple site.[2]

The Jews who remained in Jerusalem were not free to rebuild the temple because Babylon's policy would not permit it and because they lacked the necessary financial resources. Most local government officials were Samaritans—adversaries of the Jews who returned from Babylon (Ezra 4:1-4).

When Cyrus, King of Persia, conquered Babylon in 539 B.C. the territory around Jerusalem became a part of the Persian empire. Almost immediately Cyrus signed a decree permitting all captive people in Babylon to return to their

Themes in Haggai

homelands, rebuild their temples, and get on with their lives (Ezra 1:1-4; 2 Chron 36:22-23).

Although the biblical record is not clear, it seems that a small group of Jews left Babylon, possibly in 536 B.C. under the leadership of Sheshbazzar, a prince of Judah, to return to Jerusalem with the vessels from Solomon's temple (Ezra 1:8, 11; 5:14, 16). Evidently Sheshbazzar made an attempt to rebuild the temple soon after. But the work was soon abandoned, and for sixteen years no work was done on the temple.

Suddenly, on the first day of the sixth month of the second year of Darius, king of Persia, the prophet Haggai preached a powerful message to the governor and the high priest in Jerusalem. He admonished them to get busy rebuilding the temple (Hag 1:1-11). Within a month, the Lord stirred up the spirit of Zerubbabel, the governor, and the spirit of Joshua, the high priest, and the spirit of the remnant of the people. All of them came and worked on the house of the Lord (Hag 1:14).

What made the difference? Why would the people respond so readily to one sermon from Haggai when they had neglected the work for sixteen years? Perhaps it was his zeal and enthusiasm. Undoubtedly, he was the prime mover in the rebuilding of the temple. Perhaps the economic and political conditions were more favorable than they had been since the return. For whatever reasons, the prophets Haggai and Zechariah, along with the governor and the high priest, led the reconstruction project. The temple was finished and dedicated four years later, in 516 B.C. (Ezra 6:13-18).

As far as we know, Haggai's ministry lasted only about four months. There are four dates in his book:

1). The first day of the sixth month of the second year of Darius, Aug. 29, 520 B.C. (1:1)
2). The twenty-fourth day of the sixth month of the second year of Darius, Sept. 21, 520 B.C. (1:15a)

3). The twenty-first day of the seventh month of the
   second year of Darius, Oct. 17, 520 B.C. (1:15b–2:1)
4). The twenty-fourth day of the ninth month of the
   second year of Darius, Dec. 18, 520 B.C. (2:10, 20)

Haggai started the rebuilding and guided it through the
early, critical times of doubt, discouragement, and question-
ing. This second temple is often called Zerubbabel's temple.
It could have been called Haggai's temple because, almost
single-handedly, he initiated the work and gave it the im-
petus needed for successful completion. Then he dropped
out of sight. It is idle to speculate on what might have happened to him. There is no indication that he was around
when the temple was finished and dedicated.

Some scholars have criticized the work of Haggai, saying
that his only concern was with a building. Many fail to find
any spiritual message here at all. Oesterley and Robinson
said of Haggai, "His whole mental outlook and utilitarian
religious point of view (see 1:9–11) is sufficient to show that
he can have no place among the prophets in the real sense
of the word."[3] Recently Paul Hanson accused Haggai and
Zechariah of surrendering the prophetic word to the un-
critical service of a particular political program (the hiero-
cratic party) and leading the prophetic office down "an
ignominious path." He claimed that they gave up the revo-
lutionary element, which was an essential ingredient in
genuine prophecy "stemming from a vision of Yahweh's
order of mercy and justice."[4]

It is always difficult to assess a person's motives, especially
when that involves going back across centuries, by way of
literature. But it is not fair to say Haggai was only interested
in building a building, even though it was a temple. Haggai's
immediate goal was to rebuild the temple, but as R. J. Coggins
says, "It is also apparent that a larger context is envisaged.
God is assuring the people of his lasting presence with

59   *Themes in Haggai*

them."[5] Coggins rejects Hanson's harsh political criticism of Haggai and Zechariah. If we are to do justice to Haggai, we must recognize the significance he attached to the restoration of the temple. It was to be the prelude to even greater acts of God on behalf of his people.[6]

Rex Mason also takes issue with Hanson. He says:

> To dismiss the eschatological elements in the preaching of Haggai and Zechariah as merely peripheral, or a device to secure support, is to portray them in terms of near caricature since, as we shall see, the eschatological element is central to their message.[7]

Perhaps Haggai's understanding of the importance of rebuilding the temple may be found in the difference between Israel's idea of the function of a temple and that of her neighbors. Temples were common in the ancient world long before David and Solomon built the first temple in Israel. The lands of Egypt, Mesopotamia, and the Near East were filled with them. In those lands, temples were built as "homes" for the various deities that the peoples worshiped. People thought of their gods as living on earth on large manors or plantations or mountain tops. These "homes" were places where the divine touched the human and the ultimate source of power could be accessible to man. Man's duty, people believed, was to provide food, water, and delicacies for the gods.[8]

The idea of a temple in Israel was fundamentally different because her idea of God was different. Although Israel called the temple the "house of God" (Hag 1:2, 4, 7, 9, 14; 2:3, 7, 9), she did not think of the earthly temple as being Yahweh's primary dwelling place (1 Kings 8:23, 27, 30). Pagan temples were filled with idols. The temple in Jerusalem, except in times of apostasy, contained no image or anything representing God's being (2 Kings 23:4-14; Ezek 8:5-17).

Pagan temples were places of "sacred" prostitution associated with fertility cults. Israel's temple was to be a place of purification, cleanliness, and holiness. Pagan temples were places where sacrifices were offered to appease the wrath of the gods and to cultivate their favor. In Israel, sacrifices in themselves had no power or value apart from the worshiper's actions and attitudes in the sight of God.

Classical prophets often berated people who broke the covenant, violated the Ten Commandments, and then came to the temple to offer sacrifices, thinking they would be delivered. Jeremiah said:

> Behold, you trust in deceptive words
> to no avail. Will you steal,
> murder, commit adultery, swear
> falsely, burn incense to Baal,
> and go after other gods that you
> have not known, and then come and
> stand before me in this house, which
> is called by my name, and say,
> 'We are delivered!'—only to go on
> doing all these abominations? (Jer 7:8-11 RSV)

The temple in Jerusalem was, in some sense, a royal sanctuary. It was built by a king and, at least in part, financed by kings. Temple sacrifices and worship, in a proxy sort of way, were for the benefit of the entire covenant community. But the temple had problems. It was often politicized. Kings of the north and south tried to control the temple personnel and service for their own causes.

When Assyria took control of Judah in 735 B.C., foreign gods, cult objects and pagan practices prevailed in the temple. The temple was destroyed in 586 B.C.—an event some classical prophets had predicted (Mic 3:12; Jer 7:14). R. E. Clements said that Jeremiah "seems to foresee no rebuilding of the temple, nor any need to do so."[9] Jeremiah predicted that the ark would not be made again "because all of Jerusalem would become God's throne" (Jer 3:17).

But the burned-out hull of the old temple and Ezekiel's vision of the restored temple at the end of his book (chs 40–48) were the necessary ingredients the Spirit of God used to inspire Haggai to lead in the restoration of the temple.

The book of Haggai is brief. It has only two chapters and thirty-eight verses. It is made up of a framework and the oracles of Haggai reported in the third person. The framework includes the superscription, and such descriptive statements as "and the word of Yahweh came by the hand of Haggai the prophet" (1:3). Statements about dates and situations (1:12, 15; 2:1, 10, 20) were also part of the framework of the book. The first section (1:1-11) rebukes the people for their failure to rebuild the temple and challenges them to do it now. The second section describes the remarkable positive response of the people to Haggai's first sermon (1:12–15a). (Within a month, the people were at work rebuilding the temple.) The third section indicates some discouragement and disappointment in the early days of rebuilding (1:15b–2:9). The last two sections of the book talk about the pervasive, contaminating power of evil (2:10-19), and the prince of God's new kingdom (2:20-23).

We have seen that "rebuilding the temple," though a major theme of Haggai's, was not his only one. David Peterson has pointed out that Haggai was also concerned with the people's psychological response to construction, with priestly responsibility, and with civil order.[10] Looking at the book of Haggai in its present form, we may detect several significant themes: 1) a realistic view of the past, 2) a dissatisfaction with the present, 3) a sense of divine calling, and 4) a vision of a bright future.

Haggai lived near the end of the Old Testament period and had a sense of history. He knew about Israel's exodus from Egypt (2:5), an event that occurred at least 750 years earlier. He knew about the promise God made to Israel at that time (2:6). He was familiar with the former glory of the house of the Lord (2:3,9). He was also acutely conscious of the fall of Jerusalem, the destruction of the temple, and the end of the monarchy (2:20-23).

Although Haggai was familiar with his people's past, he did not dwell on it or live in it. He learned from the past. He saw the judgment of God on the people for their failure to rebuild the temple (1:9-11). He learned that it was Yahweh who gave the rain and withheld it (1:11). He insisted that it was Yahweh who gave the oil, wine, and produce and withheld them (1:11). It was Yahweh who smote the produce with blight, mildew, and hail, but the people did not repent or turn back to the Lord (2:17). This passage reminds one of the words of Amos "I smote you with blight and mildew, yet you did not return to me, says the Lord" (Amos 4:9). Evidently Haggai was familiar with a passage in Jeremiah about Jehoiachin being God's signet ring (Hag 2:23; see Jer 22:24).

Haggai's view of the past was informed and realistic. Anyone who ignores the past does so at his own peril. He knew about the good times and bad times. He also knew that one cannot live in the past or bring it back. One should learn from the past and build on it.

A dissatisfaction with the present

The Lord had been displeased with Israel in the past and brought judgment on them (1:10-11). God was still displeased with the people, but he said that if they would go up to the mountain and bring wood and build "the house" he would take pleasure in it (1:7).

Haggai, too, was certainly dissatisfied with the present conditions in Jerusalem. The people were living in "paneled" houses they built for themselves, while they left the house of God in ruins (1:4, 9; 2:3). The people said it was not time to rebuild the Lord's house (1:2). Perhaps they thought the seventy years of Jeremiah's prophetic clock had not expired. Or they may have been waiting for more favorable economic or political conditions. It was a time of high inflation and low wages (1:6). The people were never satisfied and never had enough. It was a time of great expectations and devastating disappointments (2:3). It was a time when the work of people's hands was unclean (2:14) and a time of empty barns and barren fruit trees (2:19).

Haggai and his people were dissatisfied with the present. Dissatisfaction with the present can be a good thing. The prodigal son would have remained in the pig pen if he had not developed a dissatisfaction with his present situation. A person will probably not change or do anything to improve his lot as long as he is satisfied with his present circumstances. But one does not have to be a prodigal to be dissatisfied with the present. Dissatisfaction with the present seems to be an inherent characteristic of man.

Wolfhart Pannenberg said that people differ from all other creatures in that they are "open" to the world: "Men do not find lasting rest even with their own constructs." A person's "destiny" moves beyond culture, creation, and the world. Man is dependent on something that escapes him as often as he reaches for fulfillment. "In his infinite dependence," Pannenberg continued, "he presupposes with every breath he takes a corresponding, infinite, never ending, other worldly being before whom he stands."[11] The New England author and physician, Oliver Wendell Holmes must

have been thinking about the ceaseless human search for
something new and better when he wrote:

Year after year beheld the silent toil
That spread his lustrous coil;
Still as the spiral grew,
He left the past year's dwelling for the new,
Thanks for the heavenly message brought by thee,
child of the wandering sea.
Build thee more stately mansions, O my soul,
as the swift seasons roll!
Leave thy low-vaulted past!
Let each new temple, nobler than the last,
Shut thee from heaven with a dome more vast,
Till thou at length art free,
Leaving thine outgrown shell by life's unresting sea.[12]

Haggai was dissatisfied with the ugly ruins of the first
temple, which, like a scar or wound, marred the landscape of
Jerusalem. The people had walked around the ruins and had
lived with them for almost seventy years. Now an overwhelming sense of dissatisfaction with the current condition
came over the prophet and his people. That sense of dissatisfaction led the prophet to a sense of a divine call.

A sense of divine calling

Haggai's sense of a divine call did not come through some
dramatic spiritual or ecstatic experience such as those of Isaiah, Ezekiel, or the apostle Paul. His call may have come
through a feeling of protest or outrage over the neglect of the
temple and over his people's satisfaction with mediocrity.

At first, Haggai seems to have been a lone voice crying in
the wilderness, "Build the temple of the Lord." But he was

not speaking or acting alone. He was speaking the word of Yahweh of hosts and was doing what God sent him to do (1:12). Five times we are told that the word of the Lord came to, or by, Haggai (1:1, 3; 2:1, 10, 19). Most of Haggai's specific messages are introduced with the words, "Thus says Yahweh of hosts (1:2, 5, 7, 9, 13; 2:4, 5, 6, 7, 8, 9, 11, 17, 23). The expression "Yahweh of hosts" may refer to Yahweh as the God of the hosts of heaven, meaning the stars or angels. Sometimes it refers to the hosts in God's army. In any case it emphasizes Yahweh's power and greatness. The name Yahweh occurs thirty-four times in this book's thirty-eight verses. Such frequent use of the name for God implies that a constant sense of God's presence dominated Haggai's ministry. Haggai was a "driven" man on a mission for God.

The people's quick positive response to Haggai's message indicated their conviction that Yahweh had sent him (1:12). This positive response to Haggai's preaching stands in stark contrast to the people's rejection of the messages of pre-exilic prophets. Haggai's dynamic messages of rebuke, challenge, encouragement, instruction, and hope, accompanied by the Spirit of God, convinced his hearers that God had sent him. God's hand was upon him, but he was no "visionary."

A vision of the future

Haggai was no visionary. He did not describe any grand theophanies or experiences with God. He was a rather mundane, functional, and practical person. His aims and goals were primarily immediate ones. Rebuilding the temple was only the first, necessary step in ushering in the new age of the kingdom of God. Haggai knew that what he was building was in no way comparable to Solomon's temple. There was no cedar from Lebanon, no skilled workers from Tyre (cf., 1 Kings 7:13), no gold or silver from the spoils of David's wars, and no fine-twined linen to use.

But Haggai believed that the future glory of this "house" would exceed its former glory. He knew that when the temple was done, God would take pleasure in it, and he would appear in his glory (1:7). He knew that the ingrained evil would someday be cleansed, and God's blessings would be visible to everyone (2:19). Haggai believed that someday God would shake the heavens and the earth, overthrow the thrones of kingdoms, and bring in his own kingdom (2:23). Haggai said that the signet ring that had been removed from the hand of Jehoiachin would someday be placed on the hand of a "son of David" (2:23), indicating that God was not permanently abandoning the line of David.

Was Haggai a visionary? The word "vision" does not occur in his book. We are impressed by his bustling activity and his ability to get things done. Zechariah was a man more likely to see visions and dream dreams. "Haggai will handle the hammer and nails," Paterson said, "but Zechariah will supply the blueprints of Utopia."[13] Nonetheless, Haggai spoke about "God appearing in his glory" (1:8); about the silver and the gold belonging to God (2:8); about the latter glory of this house being greater than the former; and about God giving "peace," *shalom*, in this place (2:9). All of those things are objects of vision.

The temple was built and dedicated in 516 or 515 B.C. Nothing is said at that time about Haggai's vision or his work. God's visible "glory" and the people's prosperity did not return. As years passed with the hopes of God's visible presence still unfulfilled, a doctrine grew up of necessary things lacking in the second temple. Several lists emerged, and they were not all alike. But most lists agreed on one prominent missing thing: the Shekinah, the rabbinic belief of the divine presence. As Ronald Clements says, "The most vital feature of all [the Shekinah] was lacking."[14]

This sense that something was missing from the second temple apparently goes back to the time of its rebuilding.[15]

Men could refurbish the material structure, but only God could bestow his presence. The postexilic period of Israel's history emphasized a growing transcendent aspect of the divine nature. God was conceived as the universal Lord who could not be limited to one place and one time. Clements says, "No wonder that some Jewish and Christian writers transferred the whole hope of the divine presence in a perfect temple on Mount Zion to the realm of heaven."[16]

One of the questions left unanswered in the Old Testament was, "Will God indeed dwell on the earth?" (1 Kings 8:27 RSV). A temple was only part of the answer. When Jesus said, "'Destroy this temple, and in three days I will raise it up'" (John 2:19 RSV) he was speaking of his death and resurrection as evidence of the Incarnation. This claim of Jesus to build a new temple was one of the criticisms leveled against him by his Jewish contemporaries. An interesting note added to 2:9 in the Septuagint says, "And peace of soul as a possession to the creator of the restoration of this temple."[17] The LXX annotator changed the interpretation of the word *shalom* from the material to the spiritual. The Greek word for "restoration" is *anastēsai* the word for "resurrection." Haggai saw a glimpse of the glory that was to be. Perhaps he understood it primarily in physical and material terms. Later readers knew it mainly as spiritual glory.

7   THEMES IN ZECHARIAH

This is the word of the Lord to Zerubbabel:
Not by might, nor by power, but by my Spirit,
says the Lord of hosts. (4:6 RSV)

Introduction

The book of Zechariah is one of the most neglected books
in the Bible. Elizabeth Achtemeier says, "Zechariah is one of
those books of the Old Testament to which we usually give a
passing glance."[1] Almost nothing in it is obvious. The passages chosen from it for some lectionaries (2:10–13; 8:3–12,
16–17) are not from the troublesome visionary section.
"They seem," continues Achtemeier, "neither necessary nor
profitable for the life of the church."[2]

Although the book of Zechariah is obscure in many places,
and the difficulty in interpreting it is enormous, that difficulty should not intimidate the reader. It is worth remember-
ing that this book is quoted more frequently in the New
Testament than most Old Testament books. Quotations from

or allusions to parts of Zechariah occur more than seventy times in the New Testament, primarily in the Gospels and in Revelation.

Some of the book's difficulty arises from questions concerning its date, authorship, and unity. The idea that the prophet Zechariah wrote the whole book was generally assumed until 1638, when Joseph Mede, a pious and learned Cambridge theologian, pointed out that Matthew 27:9 quotes Zechariah 11:12 as coming from Jeremiah rather than Zechariah.[3] This was the beginning of 350 years of scholarly debate about the dates and background of the materials in the book of Zechariah. There seems to be a distinct break between chapters 8 and 9. Most scholars divide the book into two main parts: 1-8 and 9-14. Although these two parts have similarities, they also have significant differences.

Major differences between the parts involve kinds of language, references to specific people and specific dates, and the importance of the temple:

- In chapters 1-8, people's names are prominent. They include: Darius, king of Persia; Zechariah, son of Berechiah; Joshua, the high priest; Zerubbábel, the governor; Heldai, Tobijah, Jedaiah, a committee of exiles; and Josiah, a local citizen. In chapters 9-14, the only proper name is "David" (12:8).
- In chapters 1-8, three specific dates are found (1:1, 7; 7:1). In chapters 9-14, there are none. The only term used to signal a time frame is "in that day."
- In chapters 1-8, references to the rebuilding of the temple occur often enough to constitute what may be the central theme of those chapters. In chapters 9-14, the temple is mentioned only three times (11:13; 14:20, 21), and then not prominently.
- In chapters 1-8, the language and literature are primarily prose and contain eight vision accounts. In chapters

9-14, all is poetry and no traditional vision accounts are found.

- In chapters 1-8, the pages are full of references to angels. In chapters 9-14, no angels appear.
- In chapters 1-8, the role of the priest is prominent. In 9-14, no priest is mentioned.
- In chapters 1-8, the role of the prophet is similar to that of the classical prophets. In chapters 9-14, the role of the prophet has ill repute and is compared to that of a person with an evil spirit (13:2).

Even though major differences exist between the two parts of the book, significant similarities, as mentioned, exist between them as well. The two parts share such common themes as the importance of Jerusalem and Zion; God's universal sovereignty; the necessity for, and provision of, divine cleansing; covenant promises and curses; evidence of tension between various groups; and the role of the humble (servant or shepherd) Messiah.

These common themes have helped some scholars see a unity in the book—even though it may have passed through different hands and different periods of refinement and editing before coming to its final form. The first eight chapters of Zechariah are a "carefully crafted document," according to Achtemeier. She says of them, "Nothing is out of place in the text or needs to be rearranged."[4] Peter Craigie noted that if the two parts of the book come from separate persons, "the fact that an editor has bound them together must not be overlooked."[5]

We must recognize the striking differences in the book, but we must also admit the presence of unifying themes. Therefore, we will consider the biblical themes of the entire book and not the different themes in its two separate parts.

Various dates have been suggested for the different parts of the book. Those dates range from the seventh century B.C.

Themes in Zechariah

to the second century B.C. There is a growing trend, however, to see the book as a unit and to assign the whole book to the last part of the sixth century B.C. We agree with Achtemeier that "there is no reason to assign them [chs 9–14] to a period other than the last half of the sixth century B.C.[6]

A cursory reading of this book shows the obvious differences between the sixth-century prophecy of Zechariah and eighth-century prophecy represented by Amos and Hosea. These latter books were addressed to Israel before the fall of Samaria. They emphasized justice, mercy, righteousness, and covenant loyalty. They had little that was good to say about the temple, priests, and sacrifices. However, sixth-century prophecy, as seen in Zechariah, considers as major themes the restoration of Zion, the temple, land, and the priesthood. Only three brief passages in Zechariah treat what we call ethical concerns (5:3–4; 7:9–10; 8:16–17). The work of the eighth-century prophets was anchored in history; the words of Zechariah are visionary and ambiguous. The reader of Zechariah constantly needs an interpreting angel. The book directs attention toward an apocalyptic "end time."

The difficulties in interpreting the book of Zechariah extend to the search for major biblical themes. Major themes of earlier books such as the Exodus, Creation, covenant, judgment, and hope are present in Zechariah, but they are not dominant. Newer themes—such as the restoration of Zion, the temple, fasting, the nations, the branch, and shepherds—recur throughout. The question of the relationship of the book's two parts also makes the search for themes more difficult. But the themes of the book as a whole should be considered. Therefore, we will summarize the message of Zechariah around four general motifs: (1) the former prophets and repentance: a look back; (2) night visions and the new Jerusalem: a look above; (3) fasting or feasting: a look around and within; and (4) the nations and the Messianic Age: a look ahead.

The former prophets and repentance: a look back

Zechariah begins his book with a look back to the times of "fathers" and the "former prophets." Zechariah is the only prophet to use the expression "former prophets" (cf. 1:4; 7:7,12). However, similar expressions are found in Jeremiah 28:8, Ezekiel 38:17, and 2 Chronicles 24:19 and 30:6-9. Later prophets and writers appealed to the words of the previous prophets to authenticate and reinforce their own words and works.

The book of Zechariah also begins with a command to repent (v 3). The reason for the command to repent was that the word of the Lord came to the prophet saying, "Yahweh raged against your fathers" (vv 1-2). The word for "rage," often translated "very angry," carries the idea of "an outburst or a fit of anger" (Isa 8:21; 2 Kings 3:27). The former prophets had commanded the "fathers,"

> Return to me, and I will
> return to you, says the
> Lord of hosts. (1:3 RSV)

The Lord had been angry with the fathers because of their disobedience. He commanded them to repent and they refused.

> "But they refused to listen, and gave a stubborn
> shoulder and their ears were heavy of hearing.
> And they made their heart like a diamond from
> hearing the Torah and the words that Yahweh of
> hosts sent by his spirit, by the hand of the former
> prophets. And there was great anger from Yahweh
> of hosts." (Zech 7:11-12)

But God does not keep his anger forever (Isa 57:16; Ps 30:5). God never closes the door to the person who will "return" to him. The invitation to return to God in repentance is always open. Jesus said, "Behold I stand at the door and knock, if any one hears my voice and opens the door, I will come in to him and eat with him, and he with me" (Rev 3:20 RSV). A prophet of the Exile said,

> Seek the Lord while he may be found,
> call upon him while he is near;
> Let the wicked forsake his way,
> and the unrighteous man his thoughts;
> Let him return to the Lord that he
> may have mercy on him,
> and to our God, for he will
> abundantly pardon. (Isa 55:6–7 RSV)

The expression "seek the Lord while he may be found" does not mean that "it is now or never," or that Yahweh cannot be found at any other time. It means that this is a very opportune time to seek him.

Zechariah's call for repentance uses the example of the fathers. The former prophets said to the generation before the exile, "Return to Yahweh and he will return to you." But the fathers refused and judgment came. The fathers and the prophets died. But around the feet of Zechariah and his hearers the rubble, the ruined walls, and a "bombed-out" temple were grave reminders that God's word is true and endures forever. Now another prophet, Zechariah, speaks to the generation after the Exile the same message, "Return to me and I will return to you."

D. L. Petersen says, "What it took disaster to teach their fathers, they may learn without such punitive measures. But they do need to turn, just as their fathers finally did."[7] Peter Craigie called this passage "An Old Message for A New Age." The new day was about to dawn, but its dawning depended on the people's turning from "their evil ways and evil deeds"

(1:4). We cannot have a new society without new people. Unless past sins and rebellion are remedied, there will be no new day. Unless the lesson of the "fathers" is learned and put into practice, the people will go on like they are. We need to look back to our mistakes and those of our fathers, correct them, and return to God.

Night visions and the New Jerusalem: a look above

A series of eight night visions follows the first oracle about repentance. These night visions, along with attached oracles to some of them, form the core of the first part of the book. Vision reports are nothing new in prophetic materials. Amos, Isaiah, Jeremiah, and Ezekiel all report visions of God or visions from God. However, these eight visions in Zechariah are reported as having occurred in a single night. D. L. Petersen defends the view that all eight visions occurred in one night, saying that there is unity and progression among the eight vision accounts.[8]

There seems to be progression within the series from the evening or twilight in vision one to the sunrise in vision eight. The fifth vision may have happened about midnight because Zechariah seems to have been in a deep sleep (4:1) and the interpreting angel had to wake him. The eighth vision occurred possibly at sunrise (6:1) and may imply that a new day was dawning for Judah and the world.[9]

Gerhard von Rad says that Zechariah regarded himself as placed exactly at the point of a sudden, great, critical change in history. The Lord was coming from his temple between two mountains (6:1; cf. 2:16, 8:3, 9:1-10). The night was far spent. The day is at hand. The temple will be built. The adversaries will be defeated (1:18-21). Prosperity will become a reality (8:10-12). "The morning has come."[10]

We must remember that the bringing in of this new day will be the work of God. Two verses in Zechariah are especially important at this point: "Be silent, all flesh before the Lord; for he has roused himself from his holy dwelling" (2:13), and "not by might, nor by power, but by my Spirit, says the Lord of hosts" (4:6). E. Achtemeier says the words of 2:13 encompass the message of Zechariah 1-8: "The Lord of hosts, the ruler of the universe has set out on a new course of action."[11] All flesh should be silent before him (see Hab 2:20; Zeph 1:7), because he is "rousing himself," "he is preparing to act" and that action will change the course of history. The second significant verse (4:6) also emphasizes that God's plan will not be achieved through military might or human power. Such power cannot bring in the new society or a new age. Only the Spirit of God can overcome any great mountain of opposition (4:7).

One great mountain that must be removed before the kingdom of God comes in its fullness is the mountain of sin and uncleanness. God removes the dirty clothes and the iniquity of the high priest (3:4). He will remove the guilt of the land in one day (3:9). In vision 6 he destroys the houses of thieves and liars (5:1-4) and in the seventh vision he removes "wickedness" (represented by a woman in a basket) to Shinar (5:5-11). He will open a fountain for cleansing the sin of the house of David and inhabitants of Jerusalem (13:1).

In the eighth and final vision, four chariots came out between the two bronze mountains (6:1-3) as messengers and warriors of God. The colors of the horses seem to have no special significance here. They are sent to patrol the whole earth (6:7). Then Zechariah is told that those who went to the north country have "set my Spirit at rest" (6-8). The horse patrol described in the first vision found the earth at rest, but that rest was a disappointment to those expecting a world upheaval that would result in the coming of the new age. It was a rest imposed by the military powers of this world. John Calvin called it an "accursed happiness" because the order is not God's order, and the tranquility gained is at the expense of God's people and plan. It is possible to create a false peace at home or in society, and call it good, when in reality "there is no peace" (Jer 6:14; 8:11).

The north country often represented evil in the Old Testament because almost all invaders of Israel came from the north, and because the dwelling place of pagan gods was in the north. The foe in the north is completely defeated. It is as though we are watching the last act of a play in which all tensions and conflicts have been resolved.[12] The night visions showed Zechariah the secret of the Power of the universe. Like the psalmist, he looked up and said:

> I lift up my eyes to the hills.
> From whence does my help come?
> My help comes from the Lord,
> who made heaven and earth. (Ps 121:1 RSV)

Fasting or feasting: a look around and within

After the work on the temple had continued for two years, a delegation came to Jerusalem, probably from Bethel, to ask the priests and the prophets if they should continue "to weep and mourn" in the fifth month. They had been doing so for several years (7:1-3), evidently in memory of the destruction of the first temple.

But fasting is not a major theme in the Old Testament. There is no law of fasting in the Torah, with the possible exception of Leviticus 16:29. The earliest report seems to be Judges 20:26. There are several references to fasting in the books of Samuel, Kings, Chronicles, Ezra, Nehemiah, Esther, and Daniel. Among the prophets, Isaiah (ch 58), Jeremiah (14, 36), Joel, Jonah, and Zechariah mention it. There are three references to fasting in the Psalms (35:13; 69:10; 109:24). Most of these references imply that abstinence from food, drink, work or sex may accrue merit before God.

Zechariah's response to the question of the continuation of fasting was to ask the delegation three other questions: (1) Did you fast for God or for yourselves? (2) Did you eat and drink for yourselves? (3) What did the former prophets say about fasting? It seems that Zechariah accused the people of fasting or feasting for selfish motives. He implies also that the former prophets were more interested in justice, truth, honesty, and kindness than in any ritualistic abstinence (7:7–10; 8:19).

Fasting, in and of itself, has no spiritual value. Only as it provides time for soul searching or as it leads to a change in attitude and conduct is it of intrinsic value. Jesus fasted forty days in the wilderness but it was not his abstinence from food that had intrinsic value. It was his clearer understanding of his messiahship that was significant in that experience. The Pharisee lifted up his eyes and prayed, ". . . I fast twice a week" (Luke 18:12). But it was the publican, not the Pharisee, who was justified. Whatever we do, we should do all for the glory of God and not for selfish gain. Zechariah said the time would come when there would be no need to fast. "The fast of the fourth month, and the fast of the fifth, and the fast of the seventh, and the fast of the tenth shall be to the house of Judah seasons of joy and gladness and for happy festivals; therefore love truth and peace" (8:19 RSV).

But it was not feasting time yet, either. Economic hardships, divisions, and strife among the people continued to plague the community. The expression 'am ha'ares, "people of the land" may indicate that some of the people were holding land that others claimed. Ezekiel 11:15-17 (RSV) speaks of a struggle for title to some lands between those who returned from exile and those who remained behind.

In another place, Zechariah describes the dire conditions in the land before the foundations of the temple were laid. He said, "For before those days there was no wage for man or beast, neither was there safety from the foe for the one going out or coming in; for I set everyone against his neighbor" (Zech 8:10; cf., 2 Chron 15:5). Unemployment was high. The streets and highways were not safe. Every man was pitted against his neighbor. But soon, fasting would turn to feasting. God was rousing himself (2:17). He would not deal with the remnant as in former days when he scattered them among the nations (8:11; 7:14). Rather than sowing their seeds in a time of fear, the people would sow in a time of peace, and they would reap an abundant harvest (8:12).

> May those who sow in tears
> reap with shouts of joy!
>
> He that goes forth weeping,
> bearing the seed for sowing,
> shall come home with shouts of joy,
> bringing his sheaves with him. (Ps 126:5-6 RSV)

The nations and the Messianic Age: a look ahead

Most of the Old Testament makes a sharp distinction between the nations and Israel. That distinction is not made in Genesis 1–11. But in Genesis 12 God called Abraham out of Ur and promised him and his descendants a land. He said they would be a blessing to the other peoples of the world. At Sinai, God made a covenant with Israel, one branch of Abraham's descendants. He said to Israel:

You have seen what I did to the Egyptians, and how I bore you on eagle's wings and brought you to myself. Now, therefore, if you will obey my voice and keep my covenant, you shall be my own possession among all peoples; for all the earth is mine, and you shall be to me a kingdom of priests and a holy nation. (Exod 19:4-6 RSV)

The relationships between Israel and the nations are a part of the whole story of the Old Testament. However, the focus on Israel is so great that often the nations seem forgotten. Israel knew she was a part of one human race. Yahweh was the Creator and the father of all the people of the world.[13] Some parts of the Old Testament speak of the nations as enemies to be defeated (Ezek 38-39; Zech 12-14). Other passages see them as coming to Zion to learn God's Law and to walk in his ways (Isa 2; Mic 4).

Zechariah mentions the nations many times and echoes these thoughts. At first, the nations were God's agents of judgment on Israel in exile (1:2; 7:14; 8:20). But God was angry with them because they went too far in their harsh treatment (1:15, 21; 12:9). God will defend his people against the nations (1:21; 12:2, 9; 14:2, 9, 12). Many nations will join themselves to the Lord and become his people (2:11; 8:20-23).

There seems, then, to be two streams of thought about the nations in Zechariah and in the Old Testament in general. One view is war-like. The nations attack Israel and are attacked by Yahweh (Ezek 38-39; Joel 3:9-17; Zech 12:3; 14:1-2), The other view is peaceful. The nations come to Zion to be blessed (Mic 4; Isa 2; 45:14; 49:22-23; 60:1-3; Zech 2:11; 8:20, 22-23). These two concepts stand side-by-side in the Old Testament under the umbrella of the sovereignty of God. Yahweh is sovereign over the whole earth (Zech 4:14; 12:1; 14:9). He is in control not only of Israel's destiny but that of the nations as well.

H. W. Wolff believes that the idea of the nations coming to Jerusalem to be blessed has its roots in the Abrahamic covenant. One verse in the story of Isaac and Abimelech is very similar to Zech 8:23. Abimelech says, "We see plainly that the Lord is with you" (Gen 26:28; cf., Isa 45:14; Zech 8:23 RSV).[14]

John D. W. Watts, in his commentary on Isaiah (WBC

24), points out that Isaiah announced in the eighth century that Yahweh had changed his strategy in dealing with Israel and the nations. The new strategy was that Israel's role would no longer be that of a Davidic world ruler. Israel and Judah were called to a passive political acceptance of imperial rule. Jews of the Dispersion were also to have a servant role.

Not many generations of Jews accepted the servant's role, however. Watts says, "The vision [of Isaiah] traces a melancholy recital of rejection for Yahweh's strategy."[15] Watts understands that God made a sovereign decision to change the "game plan" in the mid-eighth century. He intended by it not only to punish his people but to accomplish historical goals of his own that Israel failed to achieve. Yahweh had a vital, but different, continuing role for his people, a role more in keeping with the Abrahamic description than the Mosaic formulation. The Book of Zechariah maintains a tension between these two views.

Zechariah refers not only to the nations but also to the Messiah in his look ahead. From the beginning of Christianity some passages in Zechariah have had a messianic interpretation. On the night Jesus was betrayed he said to his disciples, "You will fall away, for it is written, I will smite the shepherd and the sheep will be scattered" (Zech 13:7 quoted in Mark 14:27 KVJ). F. F. Bruce says that there is "no doubt about the application of the passage in Mark's passion: the smitten shepherd is Jesus. Moreover, according to Mark, it is Jesus himself who makes the identification. I have no doubt at all that Mark is right in ascribing this interpretation of prophecy to Jesus."[16]

A number of passages from Zechariah are quoted or referred to in the New Testament as pointing toward the Messiah. Zechariah 9:9 is quoted in Matthew 21:5 and John 12:15. Zechariah 11:13 is quoted in Matthew 27:9. Zechariah 12:3 is quoted in Luke 21:24. Zechariah 12:10 in quoted in John 19:37 and Revelation 1:7. Zechariah 13:7 is quoted in Mark 14:27. Zechariah 14:5 is similar to 1 Thessalonians 3:13. Zechariah 14:8 compares with John 7:38; and Zechariah 14:21 with John 2:16. The evidence is overwhelming that Jesus and early Christians gave a messianic interpretation to many references in Zechariah.

It is easy, however, to read too much of the experiences of Jesus into some passages in Zechariah. F. F. Bruce quotes with approval T. V. Moore's saying that anyone who tries to interpret the "wounds between his hands" in Zech 13:6 as a prophecy of the nail wounds in our Lord's hands is guilty of "the grossest misapprehension of its meaning." Bruce adds, "it is astonishing that so capable a Hebraist as E. B. Pusey should have been capable of this misinterpretation.[17]

Helmer Ringgren believes that one aspect of the messianic hope in the Old Testament has its roots in the role of the king in the New Year festival. During that festival the king was anointed and proclaimed God's son. As time went on, the hopes expressed for the earthly king were transferred to a future king who would bring in God's universal reign of peace and justice.[18]

Paul Lamarche finds a single messianic expectation in the portrayal of the coming king (9:9-10), the good shepherd rejected by his people (11:4-17), Yahweh's representative who was pierced (12:10-13:1), and the smitten shepherd and the scattering of the sheep (13:7-9).[19]

There are at least three metaphors or figures for the "Messiah" in Zechariah:

- "My servant the *branch*" (3:8; 6:12);
- Israel's humble, triumphant king who will bring peace to the nations and whose dominion will reach from sea to sea to the ends of the earth (9:9-10); and
- The good shepherd who is rejected by his own people (11:4-17; 13:1-9).

The precise interpretation of these figures is debatable, and the reader should consult the larger commentaries for a thorough discussion of possible views. A growing number of scholars, however, interpret these figures messianically. D. L. Petersen notes that Joshua the high priest was told that Yahweh was bringing an individual, "my servant," a branch who would bring cleansing to the land in one day. The term "branch" is used to describe Jerusalem in Ezekiel 16:7. A future ruler of the line of David is called "branch" (Isa 11:1; Jer 23:5; 33:14-16; Zech 3:8; 6:12-13).[20]

Elizabeth Achtemeier says that in the passage about the crowns (6:9-15) Joshua only stands in for the coming "branch." The crowns are removed from Joshua's head and set aside to be placed in the new temple as a reminder of the coming messianic age. They remained in that temple through four long centuries until he whose right it was (Ezek 21:27) came. But as it turned out the crowns of silver and gold (6:11) became a crown of thorns. Jesus was crucified as the "King of the Jews" (Matt 27:28; Mark 15:26). Pilate recognized that he was Israel's long-awaited king (John 19:19-22). After the resurrection, his followers recognized that the crucified one had been exalted as the Messiah (Acts 2:36). He rebuilt the temple in three days. E. Achtemeier says that although Zerubbabel's temple has been destroyed, the crown that Joshua deposited in it has endured. In some Christian churches, the cross and the crown are made together "as a sign of the fact that the crown now rests on the head of Jesus Christ."[21]

8   THEMES IN MALACHI

Behold, I am sending my messenger
and he will clear the way before me.
And suddenly he will come to his temple,
the Lord whom you are seeking. (3:1)

Introduction

"Malachi is like a late evening which brings a long day to
a close," F. W. Farrar says, "but he is also like a morning
dawn which brings with it the promise of a new and more
glorious day."[1]

The book of Malachi stands last in the Minor Prophets
and in the prophetical canon of the Hebrew and Protestant
Bibles. The Jews called it "the seal of the Prophets" and
"the last of them." Tertullian considered it a link between
the old and new dispensations, "the skirt and boundary of
Christianity."

In one way, we know little about the person called
"Malachi." There is no consensus among scholars as to

whether *Malachi*, "my messenger," was the writer's name or his title. No other person in the Old Testament is called Malachi. We do not know his date, his occupation, (other than that he was a prophet), or his ancestry. But in another way, we know him well "for there breaks through his writing," as Mason puts it, "deep faith and intense pastoral concern."[2]

We may learn more about the intimate workings of Malachi's heart and mind by reading his book than we can learn about any other prophet, except Jeremiah. Jeremiah bares his soul before God and his people. We can observe the turmoil of his inner being in his confessions and accusations. Much the same is true with Malachi. His "deep faith" is seen in his conviction that God does not change (3:6), that he still loves his people (1:1-5), and that there is hope for those who fear God and "return to him" (3:7; 4:2-3). Malachi's "intense pastoral concern" is evidenced by the fact that he speaks about personal and religious matters. He is concerned with the priesthood, temple, sacrifices, and the way Yahweh should be worshiped. He is concerned about idolatry (2:11), divorce (3:16), skepticism (2:17), failure to tithe (3:8), sorcery, adultery, and the oppression of the poor, widows, and orphans (3:5).

Malachi saw the need for institutionalized religion, but he also saw that those institutions can and do pose a constant threat to the life of the spirit. Contrary to popular opinion, Malachi was no narrow nationalist or exclusivist. Malachi had a world vision of the kingdom of God (1:11, 14). He knew God's name would be feared in all nations. He knew membership in the kingdom was not a matter of birth or ancestry but a matter of fearing God's name and having one's own name written in the book of remembrance (3:16).

Rex Mason has said that at a time when the community needed to establish its own identity, the prophets of the restoration (Haggai, Zechariah, and Malachi) all kept "an openness toward God's purpose for people of other nations."[3]

Themes in Malachi

Elizabeth Achtemeier asserts that Malachi 1:11 and 14 speak of a universal kingdom. She says that these verses do not refer to the worship of dispersed Jews or pagans but "to the purpose that underlies every prophetic book: The future establishment of the kingship of God over all the earth."[4]

We can only estimate the date of Malachi. No dates are mentioned in the book. Its position of being last in the prophetic canon suggests that it is late and postexilic. The strong emphasis on priestly matters and the absence of any reference to any Israelite king also point to a late date.

The importance of the Persian governor (1:8) indicates a date in the Persian period (538-333 B.C.). There is a kinship between the book of Malachi and that of Nehemiah. The same social and religious conditions prevail in both. Tithing is stressed in both (Mal 3:7-10; Neh 10:37-39). Divorce and mixed marriage were a problem in both (Mal 2:10-16; Neh 10:30; 13:22-29). I have noted elsewhere that the book of Malachi fits the situation in which Nehemiah worked "as snugly as a bone fits in its socket."[5] Nehemiah came to Jerusalem for the first time in 444 B.C. A date from 450-425 B.C. is likely for the time of Malachi.

The literary structure and style of the book of Malachi is different from other books of Old Testament prophets. The book is made up almost entirely of dialogues or disputations. Six almost independent sections follow essentially the same format:

- First, a charge is made against the people or priests;
- Second, the people or priests question or challenge the charge; and
- Third, the prophet recites evidence to support his charge.

One writer seems to be shaping the speeches of all the participants in one vocabulary and style. Other Old

Testament writers include dialogue and disputations in their works (Job, Mic 2:6-11, Isa 28:23-29; Jer 2:23-37; 3:1-5), but no other Old Testament book consists entirely of this literary form.

In recent years, some conservative scholars have denied that the words put in the mouth of Malachi's opponents were ones they actually spoke in public.

Joyce Baldwin says, "Malachi reads the attitudes of his people and intuitively puts their thoughts into words."[6]

Charles Isbell says that the author tried to anticipate the major question or objection that an opening abrasive declaration would raise in the minds of the hearers or readers. On the basis of this anticipation, he then posed the question that he believed his readers or audience would raise. Isbell continues:

> However, though the question or objection was actually raised by the author, it was attributed to the audience. In this way it appeared that a dialogue was developing between the speaker and the audience, when in actual fact only one speaker was involved, and he alone was responsible for both points of view.[7]

This scenario of the way the speeches in Malachi origi-nated seems too "cut and dried." Pieter Verhoef is probably closest to the truth when he says:

> Whether the dialogues reflected the actual responses of Malachi's opponents is uncertain. It seems unlikely that they would have reacted in the precise terms of the dialogue. . . . On the other hand we may assume a certain reality in the minds and acts of the addressees that would correspond with the words that were put into their mouths.[8]

Themes in Malachi

Elizabeth Achtemeier has an interesting explanation for the disputational form of the book. She begins with a passage in Deuteronomy 17:8-13 which says that legal cases too difficult for local law courts to decide should be brought before the Levitical priests in the Jerusalem temple. The book of Malachi, then, is in the form of one of these court cases that has been moved from the village to the capital and tried before the priests in the temple, with the prophet playing the role of the priests. The questions found in the book are not hurled at the prophet on the street, in some Socratic setting, and they are not scholastic questions characteristic of the scribes. "Rather," she says, "they are questions asked in a court of law."[9]

The proposals for the composition of Malachi are many and continue to multiply. Fortunately, the ability to grasp the meaning and message of the book does not depend on solving all literary and historical problems surrounding it. One of the prophet's chief concerns was to reassure his people that God still loved them. Malachi lived in a time of despondency and depression. The high hopes of the returnees from Babylon were dashed on the hard rocks of droughts, disappointments, and doubts. Malachi faced a wall of apathy and indifference. Peter Craigie says, "He (Malachi) spoke of faith to a people for whom religion had become humdrum and who were lackadaisical in their observance of the ancient traditions."[10]

Malachi faced the problems of poverty, oppression, and unfaithfulness to marriage and covenant vows. Moral and spiritual laxity, pride, indifference, permissiveness, and skepticism were rife. Malachi tried to rekindle the fires of faith in the hearts of his discouraged people. Already the priests controlled the temple and the religious life of the people. They had consolidated their authority to the point that they were arrogant and covetous. Such abuse of power led to neglect of proper institutional worship, personal respect, and honor for God and his laws. Given the plight of the people and the position of Malachi, several major themes are discernible in his book which might help his people to "return." These include: (1) God's covenant love, (2) Israel's filial failure, (3) priestly malfeasance, (4) skeptical "believers," (5) God's coming messenger, (6) robbers of God, and (7) trial by fire.

God's covenant love

Perhaps the word that stands as the first word in Malachi—"God loves you"—is the word Israel needed most to hear. In a time of doubt, disappointment, and depression Israel needed reassurance that, in spite of their failures and the lack of spiritual and material blessings, they were still the people of God. The fact that God loves the world and that he chose Israel to be his servant is not expressed often in the Old Testament. The word "love" is a covenant word. It is also an election word. God chose Israel because he loved her (Deut 7:7–8) and her fathers (Deut 4:37; 10:15). God made a covenant with Israel at Sinai and promised to love her, bless her, and multiply her (Deut 7:13). Love is a domestic term. It describes the lover's attitude toward his beloved, the father's toward his child, and a friend's toward his closest companion. Love has in it the ideas of intensity, totality, interiority, and bondedness.

The amazing thing about God's love for Malachi and his hearers was its persistence. God's love had spanned the breaches of all ten commandments. It survived the Babylonian Exile. The blessings of covenant faithfulness were withdrawn because of the people's unfaithfulness, but God's love was still in effect.

The term "covenant" occurs six times in Malachi. The covenant of Levi is mentioned three times (2:4, 5, 8). The covenant with the fathers is cited in Malachi 2:10, and the covenant of marriage is mentioned in Malachi 2:14. The messenger of the covenant is referred to in Malachi 3:1. In addition to these six uses of the term "covenant," Malachi uses other terms often associated with the covenant relationship. The word "hate" in Malachi 1:3 should be understood as covenant language. When Yahweh says, "I loved Jacob," he means, "I chose Jacob"; and when he says, "I hated Esau," he means, "I did not choose Esau."[11] The word *arur*, "curse," in Malachi 1:14 and 2:2 is a covenant word. So is the word for "Great King" in Malachi 1:14. Malachi believed that God was sovereign as "the Great King," and God had made a covenant with the "fathers" and with Levi. Those covenants were still in effect, even after the Exile.

Another covenant word in Malachi is *sequllah* "special treasure" in Malachi 3:7. It occurs elsewhere in the Old Testament at the inauguration of the Sinai covenant (Exod 19:5) and in Deuteronomy 7:6; 14:2; 26:18 and Psalm 135:4. The idea is that all the earth belongs to God, but those who fear him and revere his name will be his own special possession. An Akkadian equivalent of this term has been found in some old near Eastern texts of covenant-grant treaties.[12] This indicates that the idea of "special treasure" is very old. So Malachi began his dialogue by establishing the basic tenet of Israel's faith—that God still loved her. But that love had some curses attached to it as the price of failure to keep the covenant.

Israel's filial failure

An axiom in the ancient Near Eastern world, including Israel, was:

> A son honors his father
> and a servant fears his lord. (1:6)

One of the Ten Commandments says "honor your father and your mother" (Exod 20:12; Deut 5:16 RSV). The commandment is stated in one place, "Every one of you shall revere his mother and his father" (Lev 19:3). In a time when the extended family was large and the members lived in close proximity to each other, it was important to have a respected leader for the family. One of the laws in the covenant code said, "Whoever strikes his father or his mother shall be put to death" (Exod 21:15 RSV). In Deuteronomy 27:16, a son is cursed who dishonors his father or mother; and in Deuteronomy 21:18-21 a stubborn, rebellious, disobedient son is to be stoned.

Israel is called God's son in Exodus 4:22 and Hosea 11:1. The people of Israel are frequently called God's children (Deut 32:5, 8; Hos 1:10; Isa 1:2, 4; Jer 3:14, 22; Isa 63:8-10). The kings of the line of David were referred to as the adopted sons of God (2 Sam 7:14; Ps 2:7). Israel, as the "son of God," was to show the same respect and honor toward him as an earthly son was to show toward his human father. But Israel had failed to show that respect. The people despised God's name (1:6). They offered polluted bread on the altar of the temple. They used blind, sick, lame animals for sacrifices. Priests "sniffed" at God's requirement and were weary and bored with worship (1:13 RSV). People made vows and did not keep them (1:14; 2:14). They practiced sorcery, committed adultery, oppressed the poor and disadvantaged, and did not fear the Lord (3:5).

Israel failed miserably as a son. The people did not honor God as Father. They did not "fear" or respect him as the Master and Lord of a servant. They did not offer him acceptable worship and allegiance.

Priestly malfeasance

"Malfeasance" is a modern word but it describes an ancient as well as a modern act. Webster defines the term as "wrongdoing or misconduct, especially in handling public affairs." The adjective "malfeasant" can mean "criminal." Malfeasance often occurs after a long period of time elapses during which one person or group gains almost absolute power in office. There is some evidence that the priesthood in Jerusalem became unusually corrupt during the latter days of the Old Testament and intertestamental period. Perhaps that corruption and abuse of power was beginning in Malachi's time. This was especially unfortunate because Israel's priests were primarily responsible for bringing the knowledge of God to the people (2:4-7). They were to instruct truthfully the people in the Torah, or teaching of God. They were to guide and counsel people in right living. They were to fear God and walk in his ways (2:4-7). No higher estimation of the priesthood is found in the Old Testament.

But the priests turned aside from walking with God in the way; and when they did, they caused many to stumble (2:8). Hosea blamed the priests for his people's lack of knowledge of God (Hos 4:4) and said that the punishment would be the same—"like people, like priests" (Hos 4:9 RSV). Malachi traces the trouble to the priests' failure to walk in the ways of God. They regarded worship as having little importance. They deemed the whole sacrificial system as a mechanical routine and deemed their role a tiresome duty.

The "walking with God" is more than a physical exercise. It suggests going the same way that God is going. It means agreeing with him, enjoying true fellowship with him, and worshiping him. The priests in Malachi's time no longer walked with God. Therefore, the honor and reverence due him were missing. Their hearts were corrupted (2:2), and they forfeited their right to be priests. God said, "So I will make you despised and abased before all the people" (2:9 RSV). These words should remind us of the awesome responsibility of people in God-given roles of leadership in the church.

Perhaps the priests' failure to walk with God and their nonchalant attitude toward their office led some people into agnosticism or skepticism. Skepticism led some Israelites into idolatry (2:11). They divorced the wives of their youth and married foreign women (2:11, 14). They questioned the justice of God saying, "Everyone who does evil is good in the sight of God, and he delights in them" (2:17 RSV). They said, "It is vain to serve God . . . we deem the arrogant blessed; evil doers not only prosper but when they put God to the test they escape" (3:14–15 RSV).

Skepticism was natural to Israel's religion and is found in some early Old Testament passages. James L. Crenshaw says, "Skepticism belongs to Israel's thought from early times," and it is "intrinsic to biblical thinking rather than an intruder who took Israel by surprise."[13] Abraham questioned God's justice when he asked, "Wilt thou indeed destroy the righteous with the wicked?" (Gen 18:23 RSV) and "Shall not the Judge of all the earth do right?" (Gen 18:25 RSV). Gideon asked the angel of the Lord, "Pray sir, if the Lord is with us, why then has all this befallen us? And where are all his wonderful deeds which our fathers recounted to us?" (Judg 6:13 RSV). The psalmist said, "The fool hath said in his heart, 'There is no God'" (Ps 14:1; 53:1 NKJV). Isaiah knew some skeptics in his time.

Woe to those who call evil good and good evil,
Who put darkness for light and light for darkness
Who put bitter for sweet and sweet for bitter!
(Isa 5:20 RSV; cf., 32:5–8)

Zephaniah accused his contemporaries of thinking that "the Lord will not do good, nor will he do evil" (Zeph 1:12). Skepticism is voiced throughout the Old Testament, so it

Themes in Malachi

should not seem surprising when Malachi addressed a group of skeptics in his day.

Skepticism grows out of doubt, and doubt grows out of disappointment. The expectations for the coming of the kingdom were high when the first group of Jews returned from Babylonian captivity. And when the temple was rebuilt, hopes were at their highest that the future of Israel was imminent. But promises of glory and grandeur faded as years and decades passed without fulfillment. Doubt and disappointment slipped into skepticism. No wonder some people were saying, "Everyone who does evil is good in the sight of the Lord, and he delights in them" (Mal 2:17 RSV).

Skepticism is not necessarily bad. Crenshaw distinguishes between skepticism, pessimism, and cynicism. He believes that skepticism includes both a denial and an affirmation. The negative side of a skeptic's mental outlook consists of doubting thought, but the fact that the skeptic questions a basic belief or affirmation indicates that it is "inappropriate to accuse skeptics of unbelief."[14] Crenshaw asserts that the matrix formed by the disparity between the actual state of affairs and a vision of what should be sharpened critical powers and heightened religious fervor. "Doubt, it follows, is grounded in profound faith."[15] Malachi told those "skeptical believers" that the Lord was coming, and he would separate the gold from the dross. He would reward the righteous and destroy the wicked (3:2–3; 3:18–4:3).

God's coming messenger

God's response to the skeptic's claim—that he no longer distinguished between good and evil, and that his promised coming was groundless—was that his coming was imminent and sure. God's coming would be preceded by a messenger who would prepare the way before him (Mal 3:1). In ancient times, a "forerunner" would go before the king's carriage to remove impediments and to make the ride of the king as smooth as possible. Malachi's statement probably rests on the prophecy in Isaiah 40:3-5 that one would prepare the way for the coming of the Lord.

The importance of this passage is underscored by the use of the word, "behold" two times in 3:1. The prophet resorts to irony in 3:1 when he suggests that the people "delight" in the messenger and are "seeking" the Lord. Then he asks, "Who can endure the day of his coming and who can stand when he appears?" (3:2). It is not quite clear who the messenger was. Some scholars have identified the messenger with Malachi, Elijah, Nehemiah or the angel of the Lord. The New Testament interprets the messenger as John the Baptist (Matt 11:10; Mark 1:2; Luke 7:27).

Although Yahweh's coming to the temple was to be preceded by a forerunner, his coming was to be sudden, not immediately necessarily, but at a time when it was not expected. Yahweh would come to the temple in judgment first. The priests, sons of Levi, would be purified. Cleansing must begin at the source of the pollution. Malachi had blamed the priests for most of Israel's spiritual problems. God would sit as a refiner and act as a laundry man using "fullers' "soap (3:2). After the spiritual leaders were cleansed, the people would be judged. Evidently the most common and serious sins of Malachi's time were sorcery, adultery, lying, and oppression. All of these sins were grounded in a failure to fear God (3:5). Where the skeptics claimed that God was pleased with evildoers, the opposite was true. When he came, he would judge the evildoers.

Robbers of God

The charges against the people were not all included in Malachi 3:4. The charge in 3:7 is spiritual blindness. They were blind to their sins. They did not see any need to repent or return to God (3:7). Their conscience was dulled by their long history of disobedience (3:7). They asked, "How or why should we repent?" F. B. Huey says the question should not be interpreted as a sincere desire to come back to God. The question implies, "why should we return?" or "how can we return if we haven't been away?" They were oblivious to any sense of wrongdoing.[16]

One area in which Israel was unaware that she needed to repent was in the area of tithing. Tithing was not listed as one of the Ten Commandments. There were obviously long periods in Israel's history when she failed to tithe. There is evidence that tithing was not being practiced at this time (Neh 10:30 and 13:23-29). Perhaps the Jews of this period did not think they could afford to tithe or that tithing was not important enough to worry about it. But Malachi shocked his hearers by saying that a failure to tithe was tantamount to "robbing God."

Stealing from another human was prohibited in one of the Ten Commandments. Now the prophet is accusing his people of robbing God. Failure to tithe was a measurable act of disobedience. Malachi indicates that the people's failure to tithe was the reason for curses on the land: God withholding rain and sending the plague of insects that were destroying crops (3:11). What is the relationship between people's failure to obey and keep the covenant and God's failure to send covenant blessings? Leviticus 26 and Deuteronomy 28 list a great many curses and blessings for those who break or keep the covenant. This may be what is involved here. Malachi says, "Here is one area in which you have disobeyed. You have robbed God. Now, bring all the tithes into the storehouse and see that I will pour you out a blessing until nothing is lacking" (3:10).

We should be cautious in our interpretation of this passage on tithing in Malachi. We should note first that the passage is not primarily about tithing but about the need to repent and return to God. Withholding the tithe is just one example of an act of disobedience that calls for repentance. Again, this passage is about a testing of God. Though we are not to test God (Deut 6:16; Matt 4:7), God on this occasion is willing to allow Israel to test him to prove to themselves and the world that he still loves them and is keeping his covenant. But this "is not a tit-for-tat arrangement, not a vending machine concept of God, not a bargain by which Judah makes an investment and receives a reward," Achtemeier says. [17] Tithing alone is no guarantee that material blessing will fall from heaven. Amos said that if his people brought their tithes every three days, rather than every three years, and their lives were filled with rebellion against God, he would not bless them (Amos 4:4–5). Blessings and repentance go hand-in-hand. In the Bible, religion and ethics, worship and morality, are inseparable. God in the Old Testament requires his true worshipers to have clean hands and pure hearts (Ps 24:4). In the New Testament, James says, "Religion that is pure and undefiled before God and the Father is this: to visit orphans and widows in their affliction, and to keep oneself unstained from the world" (James 1:27 RSV). Worship and morality support one another.

Trial by fire

Malachi complained of a blurring of moral and theological values in his day. Many people could not or did not distinguish between the righteous and the wicked. Community values had been totally reversed. The arrogant were blessed and the wicked seemed to prosper. People tested God and escaped any punishment (3:15). For his response to this reversal of values, Malachi moved from the present "here and now" to the "not yet" and ultimately to the "coming day" (4:1). A society may decide to abandon any distinction between good and evil, but God never does. He hears those who fear his name and writes their name in his book of remembrance (3:16), and he will spare them when he acts, as a man spares his son who serves him (3:17).

Then the scene shifts from the God who records human acts to the God who comes to judge the world. Those who have embraced evil will be burned as stubble, leaving them without root and branch (4:1). But those who fear his name will greet the coming day as the dawn. God will arise with the brightness of the sun in a world that has lived in darkness. Like calves frolicking on an early spring morning, so God's faithful will rejoice (4:2).

Malachi was not primarily concerned with the future. He was disturbed about the conditions "here and now." There seemed to be no present solution to all of the problems that faced him and his people. But he did not give up hope or faith in the promises of God. He believed that there was a difference between good and evil, between the righteous and the wicked; and he believed that one day God would come to judge the wicked and reward the righteous. Malachi was not teaching a doctrine of salvation by works. Those who would be spared would be spared because they "feared" God's name. Those who perished would perish because they despised his name.

The book of Malachi closes with two admonitions: (1) Remember the law of Moses; and (2) behold, I will send you Elijah the prophet before the great and terrible day of the Lord comes. The law of Moses, as interpreted in the New Testament, remains in effect for Christians. Elijah has come in the person of John the Baptist (Matt 11:10). Malachi said that the new Elijah would turn the hearts of fathers and children to each other and toward God. The expression "turn the heart" is a graphic way of saying they will repent and be reconciled to each other and to God.

Malachi indicates that a failure to repent will result in a curse (Mal 4:6). Jesus came preaching repentance for the kingdom of God was at hand. When the people did not repent he upbraided them (Matt 11:20). All are under a curse because all have sinned. Jesus bore the curse for all who will repent and turn to him in faith for redemption. Paul said, "Christ redeemed us from the curse of the law, having become a curse for us—for it is written 'Cursed be everyone who hangs on a tree'—that in Christ Jesus the blessing of Abraham might come upon the Gentiles, that we might receive the promise of the Spirit through faith" (Gal 3:13–14 RSV).

9 THEOLOGICAL REFLECTIONS ON MICAH-MALACHI

James Barr, writing recently in Brevard Childs's *Festschrift*, called attention again to the crisis in biblical theology.[1] Barr agreed that biblical theology is in crisis, but not because its productivity has come to a halt. In fact, articles, essays, and monographs on themes relating to biblical theology have continued unabated since Childs's *Biblical Theology in Crisis* was published in 1970. The crisis, according to Barr, lay not in the cessation of its activities but "in its loss of status, its loss of prestige, the loss of its power to persuade."[2]

One of the difficulties with the very idea of biblical theology is the difficulty of its definition. Theology means "the study of God," but Barr says the study of God should not be limited to a study of the Bible. Theology or "the study of God" should include the study of history, philosophy, psychology, the natural world as well as a study of the Bible. "Biblical theology" for some was not really theology at all because it limited its study to the biblical materials and because it simply attempted to organize the biblical materials in a descriptive way. For most systematic theologians theology is a modern critical construct and "a refining of *our* concepts of God in Christ and in the church."[3]

This chapter is not theology as Barr understands the term. It may not even be biblical theology in the common understanding of that term. It is an attempt to identify and organize the theological concepts in these seven books and to reflect on their significance then and now.

Is this a legitimate exercise? Is there enough unity within these books to talk about their "theological concepts"? Perhaps we should not be surprised if we find differing concepts in these seven books because they span a period of about three hundred years (725-425 B.C.) including the period of the Babylonian exile. The following chart shows the probable dates and chronology of these seven prophets

Micah	725–700 B.C.
Nahum	626 B.C.
Zephaniah	626 B.C.
Habakkuk	605 B.C.
Babylonian Exile	586–536 B.C.*
Haggai	520 B.C.
Zechariah	520–518 B.C.
Malachi	425 B.C.

The first four of these prophets lived before the fall of Jerusalem. They warned their people of coming judgment because of their sins. Haggai and Zechariah were among the first postexilic prophets. They were concerned with the restoration of the temple, the cleansing of the land, and with bringing in the kingdom of God. Malachi lived a hundred years after the Babylonian Exile. By that time efforts to restore the former glory of the temple and the kingdom of Israel had failed miserably.

Even though the first and the last of these prophets (Micah

---

* Jerusalem fell in 586; in 536 the first group from Exile returned to the Jerusalem region.

Theological Reflections on Micah-Malachi

and Malachi) were separated by three hundred years and each prophet came from a different background and addressed his own unique situation, there is an underlying unity to their theological concepts. It is true that some of them are more concerned with cultic matters (Haggai, Zechariah, and Malachi) than others. Zechariah may have a tinge of apocalyptic in his writing and thinking. Nahum is primarily concerned with Assyria, a foreign nation; Micah stresses the need for social justice and emphasizes the great saving acts of God (Mic 6:3-5). But basically all of these prophets have the same theology. Some common concepts that unite them are: (1) they are theocentric in their thinking and in their writing; (2) they all believed that societies and individuals bring judgment on themselves; and (3) they all believed that righteousness and peace ultimately will prevail.

Theocentric in thinking and writing

God is central in all seven of these books of prophecy. Each book begins and ends with either a word from God, a word about God, or a word addressed to God. The same name, Yahweh, is used for God in all seven books. It occurs 280 times in 38 chapters. The more general term *Elohim* is used for God 38 times. God's name was continually on the lips of these prophets.

These prophets thought of God as a person. He had a personal name. They did not use some general, abstract term such as "deity," "the divine," "the ground of all being," "the value-creating process," or the "object of ultimate concern" to refer to God. They used a particular specific name, Yahweh, because he was the one who had brought them out of the land of Egypt, out of the house of bondage (Mic 6:4-5; Hag 2:5).

They spoke of Yahweh in personal terms. They believed that God spoke to them (Mic 5:10; 6:1; Nah 1:12; Hab 2:2; Zeph 1:3; Hag 1:3, 5, 7, 9; Zech 1:4; 2:6; 7:8; 8:2; Mal 1:2). He came down and walked on the high places of the earth (Mic 1:3). He was a God who made ultimate decisions (Zech 3:8). He chose some people and things (Hag 2:23; Zech 1:17; 2:12; 3:2) and did not choose others (Mal 1:3). He loves (Zeph 3:17; Mal 1:2) and is gracious and compassionate (Mic 7:19; Zech 1:13). He is faithful (Mic 7:20), righteous (Zeph 3:5), and good (Nahum 1:7).

Not only is the God of these prophets loving, compassionate, and faithful but he is also holy (Hab 1:12; 2:20; 3:3; Zech 2:13). Because he is holy, he cannot clear the guilty or look on wrong (Nah 1:3; Hab 1:13). His wrath and anger are aroused by sins of idolatry, oppression of the poor, lying, deceit, and violence (Mic 6:10-13; Nah 1:3-6; Zeph 1:17-18; 3:8b).

All seven of these prophets seemed to assume Yahweh's sovereignty over nature, nations, and other powers divine and demonic. There are two explicit references in this material to Yahweh as Creator: "The word of Yahweh concerning Israel . . . the One stretching out the heavens, and establishing the earth, and forming the spirit of man within him" (Zech 12:1); and

> Is there not one father for all of us?
> Did not one God create us? (Mal 2:10)

Yahweh is able to control the harvests (Mic 6:15; Hag 1:6, 10-11). He and not the diviners gives the rain.

> Ask from Yahweh rain
> in the time of the spring rain!
> Yahweh is the one making the thunder clouds
> and gives to them heavy rain,
> and to each plant in the field. (Zech 10:1)

He can open the windows of heaven and rebuke the insects that devour (Mal. 3:10). His way is in the whirlwind and the storm and the clouds are the dust of his feet. He rebukes the sea and makes it dry (Nah 1:3-5). He controls the plague and pestilence, the mountains and hills, the rivers and seas, and the sun and the moon (Hab 3:5-11). He shakes the heavens (Hag 2:6, 21). He makes the earth desolate (Mic 7:13; Nah 2:10). He sweeps away everything on the earth like a flood and fire (Zeph 1:2-3). He is king of Israel and the world (Mic 2:13; 4:7; Zeph 3:15; Zech 14:16). Micah calls Yahweh the "lord of all the earth" (Mic 4:13).

Not only is Yahweh recognized as the lord of nature, but he is seen as the lord of all nations by these prophets. Perhaps all nations do not yet recognize his sovereignty but they will.

> Because the earth shall be full
> of the knowledge of the glory of Yahweh,
> as waters cover the sea. (Hab 2:14)

> But Yahweh is in his holy temple.
> Hush before him, all the earth. (Hab 2:20)

> Hush, all flesh before Yahweh, because he is rousing
> himself from his holy dwelling-place. (Zech 2:13)

Sometimes Yahweh's sovereignty over the nations is seen in his use of them to punish Israel (Mic 1:5; Hab 1:5-6, 12; Zech 14:1). At other times God shows his sovereignty over nations by bringing judgment on them (Mic 4:11-13; 5:6, 15; 7:10, 16-17; Nah 1:8, 14; 2:13; 3:5-7; Hab 2:15-17; Zeph 2:5, 13; 3:8; Hag 2:6; 21-22; Zech 1:15; 14:3).

Sometimes the nations are described as coming to Jerusalem to be taught God's Law. They will see the redemptive acts of God for Israel (Mic 7:16) and be ashamed of all their might. They will be humbled and perhaps humiliated. In an obvious recollection of Genesis 3:14 the nations "will lick dust as the serpent, like the crawling things of the earth."

They will come trembling from their dungeons and turn in dread and fear "to Yahweh our God" (Mic 7:17). This subservient role given to the nations reminds us of other Old Testament passages where the nations become servants and slaves of Israel (Josh 10:21; Isa 60:10-16; 61:5-7).

Occasionally the nations are seen as being converted and brought into the kingdom of God. Micah spoke of a time when the mountain of the house of the Lord would be lifted up above other mountains and many nations would flow in and be taught God's ways and they would walk in his paths (Mic 4:1-4). Zephaniah referred to a time when Yahweh would change the speech of the peoples to a pure speech so that "all of them [will call] on the name of Yahweh, to serve him with one shoulder" (Zeph 3:9). Zechariah said, "and many nations shall join themselves to Yahweh in that day. And they shall become my people" (Zech 2:11; cf., 8:20-23). Zechariah 9:6-7 speaks about a time when a half-breed people living in Ashdod will be cleansed and become like a clan in Judah, and Ekron like the Jebusites will become a part of Jerusalem. When Israel's new king comes into Jerusalem riding on a donkey, the implements of war will be cut off and "he will speak peace to the nations, and he will rule from sea to sea and from the river to the ends of the earth" (Zech 9:9-10). This passage, unlike Psalm 72:9 and Micah 7:17, says nothing about the nations "licking the dust."[4] Malachi 1:11, 14 anticipates a time when the name of Yahweh will be great from the rising of the sun to its setting. Zechariah 14:16 says that everyone in the nations that survive (the judgment) will go up to Jerusalem year after year to worship the king, the Lord of hosts, and keep the feasts of booths.

None of these seven prophets rises to the height of theological expression attained by other of the Old Testament prophets. Isaiah 19:23-25 (RSV) sees an equality between Israel, Egypt and Assyria.

Theological Reflections on Micah-Malachi

In that day there will be a highway
from Egypt to Assyria, and the Assyrian
will come into Egypt, and the Egyptian
into Assyria, and the Egyptians will
worship with the Assyrians. In that day
Israel will be the third with Egypt and Assyria,
a blessing in the midst of the earth, whom
the Lord of hosts has blessed, saying, "Blessed
be Egypt my people, and Assyria the work of
my hands, and Israel my heritage."

Isaiah 40–55 speaks of Israel's role toward other peoples as that of a "light to the nations" and that of a suffering servant.

God's sovereignty in the Old Testament includes nature, nations, and other cosmic powers (idols, gods, Satan, and cosmic forces represented by waters and sea monsters). Surprisingly, idolatry seems to have been a serious problem in Judah immediately before the fall of Jerusalem. Even though idolatry was prevalent, these prophets knew that idols had no real power or reality (see Mic 1:7; 5:13–14; Nah 1:14; Hab 2:18–19; Zeph 1:4–5; Zech 10:2).

There is one interesting reference to Yahweh's power over other "gods" in Zephaniah 2:11. Yahweh . . . weakened all the gods of the earth and every man will worship him from his place among the island of the nations." A comparison of the translation of this verse in the major English versions reveals a lot of uncertainty about its precise meaning. John D. W. Watts comments that "the subduing of the gods will lead to all men worshipping the Lord." Watts notes also that the word translated "islands" or "coasts" can mean "jackals," "ghosts," or "demons" thought of as inhabiting old ruins. "A major part of God's victory is over gods and demons (cf., Ps 82). Jesus' mastery of the demons was understood as a sign that 'the kingdom of God had already come.'"[5] This passage in Zephaniah does not necessarily authenticate the existence of other gods, but it does present Yahweh's claim to sole power in a language universally understood.[6]

"The *satan*" appears in Zechariah 3:1–2 as an accuser of Joshua because he was clothed in filthy garments. Joshua was the high priest in Judah and his filthy garments disqualified him from serving as priest before the Lord. "The *satan*" appears to be a member of the heavenly council and is rebuked by Yahweh. Yahweh is sovereign over all members (angels) of his heavenly council here just as he is in Job 1–2. The role of Satan in the Old Testament is the subject of much current debate. A growing amount of literature is available on the subject.[7] Although many issues about Satan in the Old Testament are still being debated, it is clear that this passage in Zechariah presents Satan as a celestial figure who accuses Joshua before Yahweh and the heavenly council and who is rebuked by Yahweh the sovereign Lord.

One further indication of Yahweh's sovereignty over "evil" is seen in his victory over the "waters" and the "sea" in Habakkuk 3. "Waters," "seas" and the "floods" are often used in Near Eastern literature—including the Old Testament—as symbols of the forces of chaos. Psalm 93:3–4 describes Yahweh's power over the waters.

> The floods have lifted up, O Lord,
>   the floods have lifted up their voice,
>   the floods lift up their roaring.
> Mightier than the thunder of many waters,
>   mightier than the waves of the sea,
>   the Lord on high is mighty! (RSV)

This same theological concept of God's sovereignty over "chaos" or "evil" represented by waters is seen in Psalms 18:4, 16; 46:1–3; 65:7; 69:1–2; 74:12–15; 77:16–19; 104:6–9; and in Job 38:8–10 and Revelation 21:1. All seven prophets were theocentric in their thinking and writing.

Theological Reflections on Micah-Malachi

Societies and individuals bring judgment on themselves

The one overriding message of these seven books—other than "Yahweh is sovereign"—is that "evil is doomed." The very first book, Micah, begins by warning the peoples of the world that Yahweh is coming to bring judgment on the earth. Specifically he says that Samaria and Jerusalem will experience judgment because of their sins (Mic 1:1-6).

The second book, Nahum is an eloquent expression of Yahweh's outrage against the dominant world power, Assyria, for her cruel and ruthless treatment of slaves and captive people. She piled up excessive treasures of gold, silver, and precious things at the expense of her victims (Nah 2:9). She was guilty and vile, full of lies, booty, and plunder. She plotted evil and counseled villainy (Nah 1:11, 14; 3:1). Can it be that nations and individuals in the ancient world did not believe in the judgment of God? Did they believe they could act with impunity? Did they believe that "might makes right" and there was no "payday some day?" If they did, that was a drastic mistake according to these prophets. Micah said that Samaria would become a heap in the field (Mic 1:6). Nahum said that Nineveh was no better or stronger than Thebes, the capital of Egypt. Thebes was destroyed, so Nineveh would be also. Habakkuk said that God had already appointed a day for the overthrow of Babylon and the arrogant.

For the vision is yet for an appointed time.
It hurries to the end and it will not lie.
If it tarries, wait for it,
because it will surely come.
It will not be late,
Behold, (the oppressor) is puffed up,
his soul is not upright in him,
but the righteous shall live by his faithfulness. . . .
The arrogant man will not survive. . . .

(Hab 2:3-5a)

The clear message of these prophets is that "evil is doomed." Societies like Assyria, Babylon, and Israel as well as individuals would be judged. And the evidence is clear that they brought judgment on themselves.

Righteousness and peace ultimately will prevail

The last word of most true prophets is not judgment but hope. Most true prophets were eternal optimists because they believed in the sovereignty and the grace of God. One of the great prophets in the Old Testament, Jeremiah, was told "to pluck up and to break down, to destroy and to overthrow. . . ." Then he was to *build* and *plant* (Jer 1:10 RSV). Micah's harsh word about the destruction of the temple (3:12) is followed immediately by the promise that the temple mountain would become the highest of mountains and peoples would flow into it (4:1). Micah envisioned a time when everyone would sit under his or her own fig tree and no one would make them afraid (4:4). He said that Yahweh would not keep his anger forever because he delights in steadfast love. "He will turn and show us compassion. He will tread down our iniquities ." (Mic 7:19).

Nahum said:

> Behold, on the mountains the feet of him
>   who brings good tidings,
>   who proclaims peace!
> Keep your feasts, O Judah,
>   fulfill your vows,
> for never again shall the wicked come against you,
>   he is utterly cut off. (Nah 1:15 RSV)

Zephaniah's book ends on a note of hope:

> In that time
> I will save the lame,

and the outcast I will gather.
And I will give them praise and fame
whose shame has been in all the earth. (Zeph 3:19)

Haggai's supporters were deeply disappointed with the dismal shape and size of the temple they were building. But Haggai was an optimist. He said, "'Who is left among you that saw this house in its former glory? How do you see it now? Is it not in your sight as nothing?'" (Hag 2:3 RSV). But Haggai knew Yahweh was with them. Then he said, "The silver is mine, and the gold is mine" (2:8 RSV). The latter splendor of the temple will be greater than the former, and in this place Yahweh will give peace, shalom (2:9).

Zechariah was a prophet of judgment and hope. His book is full of words of warning, but he knew that Yahweh could remove any mountain that interfered with his purpose. Yahweh said to Zerubbabel, "Not by might, nor by power, but by my Spirit. . . . What are you, O great mountain? Before Zerubbabel you shall become a plain. . . . For whoever has despised the day of small things shall rejoice . . ." (Zech 4:6–7, 10 RSV).

Five centuries after Zechariah, the apostle Paul wrote to the Roman church in the spirit of Zechariah but with more spiritual understanding. "If God is for us, who is against us? He who did not spare his own Son but gave him up for us all, will he not also give us all things with him? Who shall bring any charge against God's elect? . . . we are more than conquerors through him who loved us" (Rom 8:33, 37 RSV).

The ultimate outcome of history according to these prophets will be a time when righteousness and peace will prevail.

NOTES

Chapter 1 Introduction

1. Gerhard von Rad, *Old Testament Theology I* (New York: Harper and Brothers, 1962), 129–305.

2. Martin Noth, *A History of Pentateuchal Traditions* (Englewood Cliffs, N.J.: Prentice-Hall, 1972).

3. Paul D. Hanson, *The People Called* (San Francisco: Harper and Row, 1987), 56.

4. David L. Petersen, *Haggai and Zechariah 1–8*, The Old Testament Library (Philadelphia: Westminster Press, 1984), 110, 128.

Chapter 2 Themes in Micah

1. For a copy of Raskin's painting and its interpretation, see Cynthia Pearl Maus, *The Old Testament and the Fine Arts* (New York: Harper and Brothers, 1954), 530–32.

2. Hans Walter Wolff, "Micah the Moreshite—The Prophet and His Background," in *Israelite Wisdom*, eds. John Gammie et al. (Missoula, Mont.: Scholars Press, 1978), 78–79.

3. For a full translation of Sennacherib's document, see D. Winton Thomas, *Documents from Old Testament Times* (New York: Harper and Row, 1961), 67.

4. Karl Menninger, *Whatever Became of Sin?* (New York: Hawthorn Books, 1973), 1.

5. Harold A. Bosley, "The Book of Micah: Exposition," *Lamentations, Ezekiel, Daniel, Twelve Prophets,* The Interpreter's Bible 6 (New York: Abingdon-Cokesbury, 1956), 925.

6. R. Mehl, "Good," in *A Companion to the Bible* (New York: Oxford University Press, 1958), 152.

Chapter 3   Themes in Nahum

1. Charles L. Taylor, "The Book of Nahum: Introduction and Exegesis" *Lamentations, Ezekiel, Daniel, Twelve Prophets,* The Interpreter's Bible (New York: Abingdon-Cokesbury, 1956), 953.

2. Raymond Calkins, *The Modern Message of the Minor Prophets* (New York: Harper and Brothers, 1947), 79.

3. Ralph L. Smith, *Micah-Malachi,* Word Biblical Commentary 32 (Waco, Tex.: Word, 1984), 63, 71.

4. *The Abingdon Bible Commentary* (New York: Abingdon-Cokesbury, 1929), 785.

5. Peter C. Craigie, *Twelve Prophets,* The Daily Study Bible Series 2 (Philadelphia: Westminster Press, 1985), 61.

6. George Mendenhall, *The Tenth Generation: The Origins of the Biblical Tradition* (Baltimore: Johns Hopkins Press, 1973), 69–104.

7. B. S. Childs, "The Canonical Shape of the Prophetic Literature," *Interpretation* 32 (1978):51.

8. S. R. Driver, *The Minor Prophets,* The Century Bible (Edinburgh: T. C. and E. C. Jack, 1906), 35.

9. James B. Pritchard, *Ancient Near Eastern Texts* (Princeton, N.J.: Princeton University Press, 1955), 291.

10. Edward R. Dalglish, *Hosea-Malachi,* The Broadman Bible Commentary 7 (Nashville: The Broadman Press, 1972), 231.

11. Craigie, 66.

Chapter 4   Themes in Habakkuk

1. John D. W. Watts, *The Books of Joel, Obadiah, Jonah, Nahum, Habakkuk and Zephaniah,* The Cambridge Bible Commentary (Cambridge: Cambridge University Press, 1975), 4.

2. F. W. Farrar, *The Minor Prophets* (London: James Nesbet and Co., n.d.), 166.

3. Ibid.

4. Donald E. Gowan, *The Triumph of Faith in Habakkuk* (Atlanta: John Knox Press, 1976), 11.

5. John Paterson, *The Goodly Fellowship of the Prophets* (New York: Charles Scribner and Sons, 1950), 135.

6. James Russell Lowell, "The Present Crisis," *The Standard Library Edition of the Works of James Russell Lowell* 1 (Boston: Houghton Mifflin and Co., 1890), 181.

7. D. M. Lloyd Jones, *From Fear to Faith* (London: Inter-Varsity Fellowship, 1953), 52.

8. Paterson, 136.

9. Roland H. Bainton, *Here I Stand* (New York: Mentor, 1956), 38.

10. Ibid., 49.

11. For a discussion of the various ways of translating this verse, see the author's commentary, WBC 32, p. 117.

12. A special form of the Hebrew verb, expressing emphasis.

13. Gowan, 84.

Chapter 5 Themes in Zephaniah

1. John Julian, *A Dictionary of Hymnology* (London: John Murray, 1907), 296.

2. *The Hymnal 1940 Companion* (New York: The Church Pension Fund, 1956), 290.

3. Peter C. Craigie, *Twelve Prophets*, The Daily Study Bible Series 2 (Philadelphia: Westminster, 1985), 108.

4. John D. W. Watts, *The Books of Joel, Obadiah, Jonah, Nahum, Habakkuk and Zephaniah*, The Cambridge Bible Commentary (Cambridge: Cambridge University Press, 1975), 155.

5. Craigie, 117.

6. James Muilenberg, "The Biblical View of Time," *Grace Upon Grace*, ed. James Cook (Grand Rapids, Mich.: Eerdmans, 1975), 33.

Chapter 6 Themes in Haggai

1. Stephen Verner, *Fire in Coventry* (Westwood, N.J.: Revell, 1964), 13.

2. H. G. M. Williamson, *Ezra-Nehemiah*, Word Biblical Commentary 16 (Waco, Tex.: Word, 1985), 46.

3. W. O. E. Oesesterly and T. H. Robinson, *An Introduction to the Books of the Old Testament* (London: SPCK, 1949), 409.

4. Paul D. Hanson, *The Dawn of Apocalyptic* (Philadelphia: Fortress Press, 1970), 10.

5. R. J. Coggins, *Haggai, Zechariah, Malachi* (Sheffield: Sheffield Academic Press, 1987), 34.

6. Coggins, 55.

7. Rex Mason, "The Prophets of Restoration," *Israel's Prophetic Tradition*, eds. Richard Coggins, Anthony Phillips and Michael Knibb (Cambridge: Cambridge University Press, 1982), 139.

8. G. Ernest Wright, "The Significance of the Temple in the Ancient Near East," *The Biblical Archaeologist Reader* (Garden City, N.Y.: Anchor Books, Doubleday, 1961), 145.

9. Ronald E. Clements, *God and Temple* (Oxford: Basil Blackwell, 1965), 102.

10. David L. Petersen, *Haggai and Zechariah 1-8*, The Old Testament Library (Philadelphia: Westminster Press, 1984), 33.

11. Wolfhart Pannenberg, *What is Man?* (Philadelphia: Fortress Press, 1970), 10.

12. Oliver Wendell Holmes, "The Chambered Nautilus," *American Writers* (Boston: Guinn and Co., 1946), 213.

13. John Paterson, *The Goodly Fellowship of the Prophets* (New York: Charles Scribner and Sons, 1950), 228.

14. Clements, 126-27.

15. Ibid., 139.

16. Ibid.

17. Ralph L. Smith, *Micah-Malachi*, Word Biblical Commentary 32 (Waco, Tex.: Word, 1984), 156.

Chapter 7 Themes in Zechariah

1. Elizabeth Achtemeier, *Nahum-Malachi*, Interpretation, A Bible Commentary (Atlanta: John Knox Press, 1986), 108.

2. Ibid.

3. See H. G. Mitchell, *Haggai, Zechariah, Malachi, Jonah* 26, The International Critical Commentary (Edinburgh: T. and T. Clark, 1912), 232.

4. Achtemeier, 109.

5. Peter C. Craigie, *Twelve Prophets*, The Daily Study Bible Series (Philadelphia: Westminster, 1984), 156.

6. Achtemeier, 146.

7. David L. Petersen, *Haggai and Zechariah 1-8*, The Old Testament Library (Philadelphia: Westminster Press, 1984), 135.

8. Ibid., 111, 138-39.

9. Joyce Baldwin, *Haggai, Zechariah, Malachi*, Tyndale Commentaries (Downer's Grove, Ill.: InterVarsity Press, 1972), 130.

10. Gerhard von Rad, *Old Testament Theology II* (New York, Harper and Row, 1965), 286.

11. Achtemeier, 108.

12. Ralph L. Smith, *Micah-Malachi*, Word Biblical Commentary 32 (Waco, Tex.: Word, 1984), 32, 215.

13. For a discussion of the question of the unity of the human race, see my article, "The Race Issue in the Old Testament" in *The Cutting Edge I*, ed. H. C. Brown, Jr. (Waco, Tex.: Word, 1969), 32-41.

14. For a fuller discussion, see Smith, WBC 32, 240-41.

15. John D. W. Watts, *Isaiah 1-33*, Word Biblical Commentary 24 (Waco, Tex.: Word, 1984), chap. 25.

16. F. F. Bruce, *New Testament Development of Old Testament Themes* (Grand Rapids, Mich.: Eerdmans, 1968), 104.

17. Ibid., 114.

18. See Helmer Ringgren, *The Messiah in the Old Testament* (London: SCM Press, 1956).

19. For a summary of Lamarche's views, see my *Micah-Malachi*, WBC 32, 179.

20. Petersen, 176, 210.

21. Achtemeier, 133.

Chapter 8 Themes in Malachi

1. F. W. Farrar, *The Minor Prophets* (London: James Nesbet, n.d.), 230.

2. Rex Mason, "The Prophets of Restoration," *Israel's Prophetic Tradition*, eds. Richard Coggins, Anthony Phillips, and Michael Knibb (Cambridge: Cambridge University Press, 1982), 149.

3. Mason, 151

4. Elizabeth Achtemeier, *Nahum-Malachi*, Interpretation, A Bible Commentary (Atlanta: John Knox Press, 1986), 108.

5. Ralph L. Smith, *Micah-Malachi*, Word Biblical Commentary 32 (Waco, Tex.: Word, 1984), 298.

6. Joyce Baldwin, *Haggai, Zechariah, Malachi*, Tyndale Commentaries (Downer's Grove, Ill.: InterVarsity Press, 1972), 214.

7. Charles D. Isbell, *Malachi* (Grand Rapids: Zondervan, 1980), 9.

8. Pieter A. Verhoef, *The Books of Haggai and Malachi*, The New International Commentary on the Old Testament (Grand Rapids, Mich.: Eerdmans, 1987), 166

9. Achtemeier, 172.

10. Peter C. Craigie, *Twelve Prophets*, The Daily Study Bible Series 2 (Philadelphia: Westminster Press, 1984), 225.

11. For a fuller discussion of this "love-hate" terminology in a covenant language, see my commentary, *Micah-Malachi*, p. 305; and Steven L. McKensie and Howard N. Wallace, "Covenant Themes in Malachi," *Catholic Bible Quarterly* 45 (1983):549-63

12. Covenants or treaties in the ancient Near East were of two kinds: vassal (or obligatory) and grant (or promissory). The grant treaty was a promise of an emperor, usually to his son or servant, of land and/or a house. In the Old Testament, God promised Abraham a land and David a house. See my commentary, p. 338, for a fuller discussion.

13. James L. Crenshaw, *Old Testament Wisdom* (Atlanta: John Knox Press, 1981), 196.

14. Ibid., 191.

15. Ibid.

16. F. B. Huey, "An Exposition of Malachi," *Southwestern Journal of Theology* 30 (Fall 1988):18-19.

17. Achtemeier, 189.

Chapter 9 Theological Reflections on Micah-Malachi

1. James Barr, "The Theological Case Against Biblical Theology," in *Canon, Theology and Old Testament Interpretation,"* eds., Gene Tucker, David L. Petersen, and R. R. Wilson (Philadelphia: Fortress Press, 1988): 3-19.

2. Ibid., 4.

3. Ibid., 9.

4. For a discussion of these passages see my commentary *Micah-Malachi*, p. 257 and R. E. Clements, *Old Testament Theology*, p. 95.

5. J. D. W. Watts, *The Books of Joel, Obadiah, Jonah, Nahum, Habakkuk and Zephaniah*, The Cambridge Bible Commentary (Cambridge: Cambridge University Press, 1975), 171.

6. Ibid., 171.

7. For a review of this literature see Peggy Lynne Day's Ph.D. dissertation at Harvard University, *Satan in the Hebrew Bible*, June 1986 (microfilm), and Rivkah Kluger, *Satan in the Old Testament* Northwestern University, 1961.

SELECTED BIBLIOGRAPHY

Achtemeier, Elizabeth. *Nahum-Malachi*. Interpretation Commentary. Atlanta: John Knox Press, 1986.

Craigie, Peter. C. *Twelve Prophets*. vol. 2, The Daily Study Bible Series. Philadelphia: The Westminster Press, 1985.

Coggins, R. J. *Haggai, Zechariah, Malachi*. Sheffield: Sheffield Press, 1987.

Limburg, James. *Hosea-Micah*. Interpretation Commentary. Atlanta: John Knox Press, 1988.

Mason, Rex. *Haggai, Zechariah, and Malachi*. The Cambridge Bible Commentary. Cambridge: Cambridge University Press, 1977.

Mays, James L. *Micah*. The Old Testament Library. Philadelphia: The Westminster Press, 1976.

Petersen, David L. *Haggai and Zechariah 1-8*. The Old Testament Library. Philadelphia: The Westminster Press, 1984.

Smith, Ralph L. *Micah-Malachi*. Word Biblical Commentary 32. Waco, Texas: Word Books, 1984.

Verhoef, Pieter A. *Haggai and Malachi*. The New International Commentary on the Old Testament. Grand Rapids, Mich. Eerdmans, 1987.

Watts, John D. W. *The Books of Joel, Obadiah, Jonah, Nahum, Habakkuk, and Zephaniah*. The Cambridge Bible Commentary. Cambridge: The University Press, 1975.

INDEX OF SCRIPTURES

Index of Scriptures

Index of Scriptures